# A Time
# Before Deception

# A TIME BEFORE DECEPTION

## TRUTH IN COMMUNICATION, CULTURE, AND ETHICS

◆ NATIVE WORLDVIEWS ◆
◆ TRADITIONAL EXPRESSION ◆
◆ SACRED ECOLOGY ◆

## THOMAS W. COOPER

Foreword by DR. FOX TREE
Epilogue by CHIEF OREN LYONS

**Clear Light Publishers**
Santa Fe, New Mexico

# For Indigenous People Everywhere

# And for my University of Hawaii and Emerson College colleagues, especially Carol, Dick, Liz, Dan, and Majid.

Clear Light Publishers, 823 Don Diego, Santa Fe, N.M. 87501

First Edition
10 9 8 7 6 5 4 3 2 1

## Library of Congress Cataloging-in-Publication Data

Cooper, Thomas W. (Thomas William), 1950–   .
    A time before deception: truth in communication, culture,
and ethics / by Thomas W. Cooper; foreword by Dr. Fox Tree.
        p.    cm.
    Includes bibliographical references and index.
    ISBN: 0-940666-59-6
    1. Communication—Cross-cultural studies.  2. Indians of   North
America—Communication.  I. Title.
    GN452.C66  1995
    302.2—dc20                                          94-43547
                                                              CIP

Cover Photograph © by Marcia Keegan; Pictograph, Cimarron County, Oklahoma.
Typography/Design/Layout by Vicki S. Elliott.
Printed in the United States.

# Contents

# Foreword

This culturally rich book, this bridge from the past to the future, reminds me of the grapes of Europe and how they were saved from extinction by being grafted onto Indigenous "American Indian" grapevine root stocks. Sometimes it becomes necessary for those of one culture to preserve the heritage of another. Each page of this book becomes a gem worthy of consideration in the preservation and sharing of knowledge.

Tom Cooper has spent many years studying, traveling, and living with Indigenous People. He seeks and finds answers to several mysteries that have their origins in the remote ancestral past. The keepers of those traditions and various symbols of logic and rational explanations are the Spirit and Power People of different nations. What might have been lost forever has been saved. From journeys of inquiry and appreciation come these treasures that are revealed to the world. Herewith are gems of different species, myriad colors, exquisite selections, and superb taste.

The destruction of so much that was the patrimony of so many Indigenous Nations has given rise to a new birth of interest. People everywhere want to know more about the ancient vanishing cultures. How did it happen that so much was lost, and what are the victims doing to preserve the essence of their creeds, convictions, and ancient traditions? The survivors of the world's greatest event, occasioned by invasion, conquest, enslavement, and extermination, have continued their mystic rituals in the face of every devastation. Tom Cooper walks in a mysterious vineyard. He gathers select items for preservation and brings them forth in this form for the palatable enjoyment of all who seek knowledge.

The long journey of initiation, of sitting alone in the wilderness, of waiting for days or months for a vision that leads to totemic inspiration or that prepares the selected one for the years of inculcation and inclusion that is conferred by the wiser elders and leaders is spared the reader. The wisdom of the Indigenous past can be enjoyed without the pain and struggle of ritual learning that usually accompanies such involvements. Wisdom is often understood and conveyed by those who understand the why of human existence and the many meanings of life. From the edge of extinction comes the saving grace of a small feast.

Tom Cooper takes you on a journey of understanding into the cosmology of Indigenous beliefs through their forms of communication. As you cross time and space toward a deeper spiritual understanding, you will be assured of the helpful hand of a worthy guide. Together you will soar above the mountains and through the valleys to observe and touch the Indigenous Circle of love for an understanding that binds the past to the present and to the future. The Circle receives that life energy and grows to include people everywhere.

The rootstocks of the Indigenous People have survived for a reason and purpose. From ancestral Indigenous rootstocks come these beautiful blossoms and special fruit for the enrichment of the world.

**Dr. Fox Tree**
Chief, Arawak Nation
Professor of Indigenous Studies,
History, and the Arts
University of Massachusetts

# Acknowledgments

In different parts of the world at the outset of Native ceremonies, Native "elders" would be acknowledged. So, too, do I acknowledge "elders" from communities who openly welcomed me into their society — Joe Archie from the Shuswap people, Rubellite Johnson from the Native Hawaiians, and Thomas Littleben of the Navajo People. They represent the 100-plus senior spokespersons for Native groups I visited.

Some of the most helpful people in my fieldwork were the chiefs and community leaders of various tribes. Charlotte Christopher, Chief Roy Christopher, Freddy Johnson, Rex Lee, Chief Bill Chelsea, Toni Archie, Elizabeth Pete, and Antoine Archie were especially helpful. Indeed, the entire bands of Shuswap People at Canim and Alkali Lakes were particularly supportive. The Rock Point (Arizona) Navajo reservation, particularly its school, offered valuable materials.

None of my on-site research would have been possible without the key liaison work of Dorothy Hughes and Eleanor Velarde, longtime friends who have spent many years working on location with their Native associates. Richard Brislin, author of *Cross-Cultural Encounters,* was also very helpful in serving as a bridge at the East-West Center, when I was a visiting scholar there meeting with Native Hawaiians and Polynesians. At Harvard, my former teachers Irving Devore and Robert Gardner pointed me toward tools to prepare for anthropological fieldwork, and the

Australian scholar Les Hiatt introduced me to valuable research on the Aboriginals.

In addition to my association with the East-West Center and Harvard University during my sabbatical, I was a visiting scholar at the Poynter Center in St. Petersburg, Florida, where I brushed up on new writing in ethics, a central thrust of my research. My thanks to all three institutions, especially to Wei-Ming Tu, Stephen Friesen, and Richard Brislin at the East-West Center; to Vlada Petric, Robert Gardner, Irving Devore, and the excellent librarians at Tozzer Library at Harvard; and to Bob Haimon, Roy Peter Clark, Don Fry, and Bob Steele at Poynter. John DeMott and several Tennessee librarians also helped me acquire valuable documents through interlibrary loan while I was visiting Memphis State University and relatives in Bolivar, Tennessee.

I could never have given this work the attention it deserves without a one-year sabbatical from Emerson College. President John Zacharis, Acting President Jackie Liebergott, David Gordon, the Faculty Status Committee, and many other colleagues could not have been more supportive in providing full leave for my research. Associate Dean Mary Harkins and David Schick provided special typing support. Throughout my travel many people provided me with an orientation to my new environment and with accommodation. These included Charles Lindsay, David and Louise DiGrandi, the 100 Mile House Emissary community in British Columbia, Ross and Marcia Marks, Gary and Gloria Brooks, David and Margaret Cooper, Laurel Cox, and my special liaisons Dorothy Hughes and Eleanor Velarde.

Much of my academic and historical research extended beyond my usual work in the corridors of communication scholarship. Among my guides to new literature, fields, and thinking were Mary Alice Donaher, Richard Heinberg, Owen Barfield, Roger Wescott, Geoffrey White, Andrew Arno, Mircea Eliade, Grace

Van Duzen, Hugh Malafry, Bob Gardner, Irv Devore, Sally Falk-Moore, Winston Smith, John Nance, Anne Wilson-Schaef, Elizabeth Bird, James Ritchie, and Lawrence Sullivan. To the many of these fellow researchers who granted me lengthy interviews, extended correspondence, bibliographic directions, or helpful leads, I express genuine gratitude.

Dr. Norman London of the Canadian Consulate and Robert Roetger at Emerson College were effective advisers in my successful application for research funding from the Canadian government. The Kaltenborn Foundation, Emerson College, the East-West Center, Harvard University, and the Poynter Center all provided useful additional support, whether financial or in-kind.

During the preparation of the manuscript, new friends brought valuable expertise to the creation of this book. These included Harmon Houghton, Marcia Keegan, Sara Held, Vicki Elliott, and Valerie Shephard of Clear Light Publishers. During the final stages of editing and proofing, my colleagues at the University of Hawaii, V.P. Carol Eastman, Dean Richard Dubanoski, Dan Wedemeyer, Elizabeth Kunimoto, and the Department of Communication were very supportive.

It was not always easy for my wife and daughter to be without "daddy," particularly when I was sleeping in tepees and nowhere near a telephone. For their patience, understanding, and loving support while I was away I offer great thanks. No one could have a more wonderful family. An extended family of relatives, colleagues, and spiritual friends have also encompassed and undergirded my work in an exceptionally generous manner. These include Michael and Nancy Exeter, Roger DeWinton, Janine Romaner, Jim Wellemeyer, Richard and Diane Friedman, Eloise and Fulton Robertson, Robert Hilliard, John and Pam Gray, my Emerson and Emissary "families," and especially my parents. At the close of Native ceremonies (and often at other times), most tribes chose to acknowledge the "Great Spirit," which they knew by many names — Wankantaka, the Old One, First Man and First Woman, Eagle, and the Sun, among others. In a material age characterized by rational analysis, many may wish to join them in acknowledging some *visible* power source, such as the sun, without which all known life would disappear. Others may join more directly with the Native form of acknowledgment by worshiping an *invisible* Creator or Divinity, whether God or Life or Allah. Ultimately, I join my Native friends in acknowledging this greater power, by whatever name it is known, not only for the existence of this book and its subject but for all Existence.

# CHAPTER ONE

*Creation of a buffalo robe. The artist is shown gesturing with his "paint brush," a tool traditionally made from the porous section of a buffalo leg bone. His son and translator of the robe sits with pen and paper in hand beside his father. Photograph by Edmund Morris, 1909. Courtesy Provincial Archives of Manitoba, Winnipeg, Edmund Morris Collection 195.*

# Introduction:
# Native Communication
# and Ethics

## With Forked Tongue

As a child I watched TV westerns in which "Indians" said "How" and "White man speak with forked tongue." The cliché "with forked tongue" meant that the new American government spoke with two meanings or "out of both sides of its mouth" to "Indians." On the one hand, promises and treaties would be made; on the other, these promises and treaties would be broken, or just as quickly amended, adjusted, or reinterpreted by government officials, soldiers, or settlers.

Although the Native Americans depicted in Hollywood movies and television shows were shallow stereotypes, the forked tongue cliché accurately suggested two approaches to communication. Settlers and soldiers were accustomed to double-dealing politicians who said one thing, but meant another. Many Native Americans, however, saw lying as a sign of insanity. "A person who does not speak truth must not know reality, and thus is to be pitied," Native elders told me. Thus some Native tribes treated their dishonest members as Westerners treat the legally insane.

This book is an attempt to uncover the neglected prong in the "fork" of communication. How did Native People communicate prior to the approach of the "white man?" If there was a "fork" in the road between "native" and "imported" communication, what were the rules, tools, rituals, and attitudes surrounding authentic Native communication? How may Hollywood stereotypes be shed in favor of a more accurate understanding of tribal peoples? Did any Native Peoples actually have a totally truthful culture (without a forked tongue) or is the notion of "a time before lying" also a myth? What communication ethic(s) characterized Native societies?

## Which Native Peoples?

To be sure, some Native cultures were as different from each other as are many individual European or Asian countries. I will make no sweeping generalizations about "all" Native or "all" industrialized societies. Indeed, few records have survived most lost tribes and civilizations, and interpretations of those records differ widely. Many groups of people are mixtures of Native and imported cultures and the blood of most, if not all, of us can be traced to more than one tribe or nation. So, as this book distinguishes between "Native" and "Western" communication, one should keep in mind that there are shades of gray, unknowns, and exceptions.

Did you ever wonder how smoke signals were used or why flaming arrows were shot high into the night sky? Have you ever asked about the "magic spells" cast by "witch doctors" and "medicine men" or the reasons "Indians" wore "war paint"? In an age when we find advertising deceptive, entertainment violent, and news sensational, might we learn from the simpler yet deeper communication practices of Indigenous People?

By "Indigenous" People, I mean all the simplest definitions of that word—"native," "authentic," "not imported," "genuine," "local," "homegrown," "intrinsic," and "natural." So, unless I am speaking of particular tribes, I am referring to tribal, oral, non-industrialized societies of all continents. Moreover, I refer to these people in their most authentic culture, prior to the outside influence of literate peoples.

It is of note that Native Nations (or tribes) of the world have by far outnumbered geopolitical "nations" (e.g., Prussia, Rhodesia, China, Canada) throughout history. The immigrant European and Asian settlers who established new "nations" (e.g., the United States, Australia, New Guinea, and South Africa) have been seen as newcomers by Native inhabitants. What Westerners call "civilized" nations may account for less than 1 percent of all the nations of Native Peoples, many of whom are extinct.

While the origins of most Native Peoples are unknown, it is likely that they, too, were originally immigrants, so new stereotypes separating "migrating" from "permanent" peoples should also be avoided. Most, if not all, tribes originally mixed and migrated.

One important observation, however, is that Native People are at home in their surroundings. Unless there is a threat to survival, most tribal people have completed their migrations. However, Western settlers continue their exodus into remote frontiers, new vacation resorts, and outer space.

## Hollywood Natives Old and New

Media stereotypes quickly crumble in the investigation of Native communication. For example, the penny novel cliché "low man on the totem pole" referred to the bottom person in a social pecking order. Actually the lowest person depicted on a Native totem pole was frequently the chief, so he could be protected by those above him. It was the guards, whether animals or tribal scouts, who sat at the top of the pole, so as to see afar and protect the encampment.

White settlers who saw long tobacco pipes at peace treaty ceremonies dubbed them "peace pipes." Yet this would be like labeling horses "war animals," if one had only seen horses ridden by cavalry, often a Native's first exposure to horses. "Peace" pipes, like "war" paint and "battle" cries, were natural parts of a social order that soldiers encountered only in special situations, such as battles and treaty ceremonies. Thus much Native communication was misunderstood, then mythified by penny novels and Hollywood, because, like these names, it was encountered out of context by members of a different culture.

More recent films like *Little Big Man* (1971) and *Dances with Wolves* (1990) have sought to demystify Indigenous People by hiring Native actors and depicting an insider's view through authentic language and customs. However, what is of real interest is what such films say about the people who make and view them. During the world wars and cold war, Westerns (and the West) needed an "enemy" to defeat; tribes ("Indians," Zulus, headhunters, prehistoric savages) were easy targets. Following the countercultural sixties and the fading of Nazi and Communist "enemies," society has been said to have turned inward, such that the fascination with alternative Native cultures has been part of a spiritual quest for identity and meaning. For example, *Little Big Man* and *Dances with Wolves* are not just the titles of films, but are the names given to their central characters adopted from White society. Such names honor core personality traits of those named. In the former, however, when Chief Dan George asks Little Big Man (Dustin Hoffman) how General Custer earned his name, there is no meaningful reply. Custer's name, like those of most soldiers and settlers, was simply inherited, almost mindlessly passed on, without discernment or rite of passage.

Recent interest in Native communication notes that there is "something behind the name," backing the ceremony, substance beneath the style. *Dances with Wolves* affirms that there was substance behind the individuals, the people, the culture, and the spirit of those dubbed "American Indians" in nineteenth-century America. In the "civilized" world, we currently speak of alienation, emptiness, hype, puffery, hollow words, empty phrases, political rhetoric, and, in the words of Simon and Garfunkel, "people hearing without listening." In the tribal world, words, dances, names, painting, intonation, carvings, blanket design, brush strokes, masks, chants—all had unique symbolism and substance. In an age of ethical quandaries, identity quests, and empty postmodernism, a culture that communicates "meaning" and a deep spiritual integrity is compelling to many.

## Environmental Significance

A return to environmental concerns also draws literate societies closer to the nonliterate world. Most Native communication was about or with the natural environment. I have spoken with elders who have communicated with owls, deer, and beavers. Some elders remember their elders' elders asking a tree's permission before cutting it down or requesting a rock's permission to relocate it. Each species of plant and animal hosted a sacred spirit with symbolic meaning which could be contacted.

Since the 1600s the Cogi People of Colombia have lived in total seclusion in the Sierras, driven from their lands by Spanish conquerors. In 1990 the Cogi broke their total isolation by inviting the first outsiders, a BBC television crew, to visit them ("the elder brother") and convey their message to the outside world ("the younger brother").

In a ninety-minute documentary, TV producer Alan Eleira

conveyed the Cogi message in "From the Heart of the World: The Elder Brother's Warning" (BBC 1990). In that program the Cogi demand that the younger brother (Western civilization) stop destroying the world. Because the Cogi work so closely with nature, they can easily determine that, as the vegetation at the top of the mountain perishes, all beneath it will vanish as well. Increasingly, we, the "younger brother," are also interested in communing with and preserving the natural world. Native perception and communication is a door to regaining natural harmony and balanced ecology.

## Heritage

Unlike the Cogi message, this book is not just for "outsiders." Many of my Native friends and associates, bemoaning a lost heritage, have asked, "Please tell us what you find out. We have forgotten the ways of our ancestors."

With respect for such tribal colleagues, I write in the hope that they, like we, may engage in what Roger Wescott calls "anamnesis, the recovery of buried memory, both individual and collective" (cited in Heinberg 1989 xx). Wescott reminds us that Greek "devotees of the Orphic Mysteries sought to offset Lethe, the traditional River of Forgetfulness, with a Lake of Remembrance, in which their initiates would bathe to regain recall of the primal cosmos and their place in it." To the extent it is successful, anamnesis not only awakens the Native to "roots" but provides a déjà vu for all societies. After all, which culture can claim to be fully autonomous? All peoples have tribal ancestors.

Indeed the gifts of Native Peoples to their modern landlords are ubiquitous. In "Indian Communication," the Native Princess Red Wing St. Cur reminds us of some little known facts:

*The coffee that you had for breakfast, the rubber on which you rode here were our gifts to this civilization. We gave civilization over 600 kinds of corn. Boston Baked Beans was a Wampanoag dish and the Indians taught the Pilgrims how to make clam chowder, oyster stew, pumpkin pie (believe it or not), cranberry sauce, corn soup and pop corn. They had developed all kinds of corn, bean, pumpkins, squash, celery, buckwheat, peppers, tapioca, potatoes, sweet potatoes, tomatoes, peanuts, chewing gum, and pineapple—it did not originate in Hawaii; rather it was grown in America and carried over the sea. (Red Wing St. Cur 1976, 355)*

But the contribution of "American" Natives is far larger than food preparation. St. Cur expands her lesson:

*Quinine is one of the many Indian medicines, and the Indians had perfected balls made of rubber which some of the early explorers were afraid of, thinking they were alive. When the explorers in South America saw the cotton fabric the Indians made, they thought it was silk. And now cotton is grown all over the world.*

*Did you ever see a lacrosse game? It is a fast game invented by the Indians; they also played hockey in South America, and marbles. In New England, we had toboggans, snow shoes, sleeping bags. In southern states the Indian used hammocks. In South America he refined gold and used it to fill teeth which he brushed. In short oral hygiene was also a gift from him. These are only a few of the Indians' gifts to civilization. (Red Wing St. Cur 1976, 355)*

It has been easy for outsiders to suggest that because the Native was "primitive," his legacy included only the physical gifts described above, not more civilized, conscious, and cultured gifts. Yet in 1936 the independent researcher Max Long wrote, "I have found that all our discoveries in psychology are things which the Kahunas [Native Hawaiian tribal healers and leaders] have used daily for centuries in the performance of magic" (Long 1978, 18). Lawrence Sullivan of Harvard University went farther than Long in suggesting that modern psychological terms such as "id," "ego," and "superego" simply echo the "multiple soul" teachings of various African and Hawaiian tribes (Sullivan interview, 1/10/91).

Such a legacy interpenetrates the "higher order" of our nominally "sophisticated" Western culture. Jane Ritchie proclaims that even the "civilized" religions imposed on Natives were derived from Aboriginal traditions. Otherwise bizarre practices, such as baptism by immersion, communion (evoking cannibalism), confirmation, and other Christian sacraments make much more sense when viewed as adapted Native rites of passage (J. Ritchie interview, 1/10/91).

Our rich inheritance from Native cultures is more than memory or acknowledgment. For many, the spirit of Native communication is inextricably woven into a perishing fabric of life that is essential to our well-being. As the Native spokesman Luther Standing Bear remarked in 1933, "when the Indian has forgotten the music of his forefathers, when the sound of the tom-tom is no more, when noisy jazz has drowned the melody of the flute, he will be a dead Indian" (1988, 56). Such sentiments by Native leadership are not simply a clinging to the implements of culture, nor are they naive nostalgia. At a deeper level, Standing Bear implies that as the sacred vibration of life is challenged, changed, or cheapened, so too are the people who utter it and their atmospheric surround. For many peoples, it is not just costumes and instruments that become obsolete with the demise of authentic communication but also the rhythms that connect humanity to the natural world and thus to a healthy and meaningful existence.

## Understanding Cultural Bias

Although I am a world traveler, I was born a white Anglo-Saxon Protestant male in a small hospital in Tennessee. My family moved every two or three years, so I became accustomed to changing cultures and lifestyles, although the people nearest me usually reinforced my own values. Although many Shuswap, Navajo, and Polynesian people have welcomed me into their societies as an honored guest, even as an "insider" in some ways, there can be no pretense that I am Shuswap, Navajo, or Polynesian.

Although empathetic, open-minded, a "blood brother," even an "honorary tribe member" to some, I write as an urban middle-class professor who was educated at Harvard University and the University of Toronto. I lived in a house or apartment for more than forty years; in tepees, huts, and reservation houses, for less than fourteen months.

For many years I studied the academic literature about cross-cultural methods and I spent part of my sabbatical preparing with experts in cross-cultural encounters. Such tools (see appendix) help the scholar to "cross" from one culture into another without importing the mindset of an outsider, one blind to the different perspective, mores, and tempos of the insider's culture. This book is committed to that approach, that is, to helping us see and hear Native communication through Indigenous eyes and ears, to "walk a mile in their moccasins."

For that reason, since many of my readers may also be "outsiders," I wish to identify some of the biases our "civilized" society often conceals when viewing Native People. The more open our minds are to appreciating underlying cultural differences, the more likely we are to fathom, if not experience, Native communication.

## ASSUMPTION #1: LITERATE CULTURES ARE SUPERIOR

The twin thrusts in our society, advanced education and the elimination of illiteracy, make it difficult to imagine that nonliterate people may be extremely intelligent, or, for that matter, to remind ourselves that literate people have created a civilization on the brink of disaster. Whatever the many gifts of literacy to society, Socrates himself warned that

> discovery of the alphabet will create forgetfulness in the learners' souls, because they will not use their memories; they will trust to the external written characters and not remember of themselves. . . . You give your disciples not truth but only the semblance of truth; they will be hearers of many things and will have learned nothing; they will appear omniscient and will generally know nothing; they will be tiresome company, having the show of wisdom without the reality. (Plato, 1868, 142)

What is significant about oral societies is that they are rich with their own oral literature and arts. Within cultures one notes the *presence* of a wide variety of communication formats, such as dance, chant, carving, sculpture, painting and oral literature, rather than the *absence* of writing and print. To label them "illiterate" or "nonliterate" suggests that they are beneath a societal norm, primitive, and backward.

Many societies, like the Cogi of Colombia, have deliberately resisted the imposition of a literate culture on their own, since they believe that print reorganizes the smoothly functioning natural order and coherence of the group. The Cogi feared that reading and writing would bring the belligerence, commercialism, and condescending values of those who used it. Preserving an oral culture is not necessarily an act of resistance, as educators and missionaries have often assumed. (In their attempt to Westernize and convert the "heathen," Westerners have wanted the unsaved to learn to read the Bible and speak English.)

Instead, there are communication values that most tribal people prefer to the linear mindset they associate with bureaucracy. As Professor Philip Peek states, "We must continually remind ourselves of the limits of literacy and the hazards of exclusively literate scholarship. For many cultures that we seek to understand, hearing is believing" (Peek 1981, 41). "Seeing is believing" is not a universally held notion. Oral societies have little experience with writing and often fear change. Moreover, for generations they have relied on spoken transactions.

Even more persuasive are the words of "insider" Mamoudou Konyate, a master *griot* (shaman) of Mali:

> *Other people use writing to record the past, but this invention has killed the faculty of memory among them. They do not feel the past anymore, for writing lacks the warmth of the human voice. With them, everybody thinks he knows, whereas learning should be a secret. The prophets did not write and their words have been all the more vivid as a result. What paltry learning is that which is congealed in dumb books. (Konyate, quoted in Peek 1981, 41)*

Ironically, Konyate is quoted in *this* book, and his words might not reach you otherwise. Yet, reading about oral societies is like reading cookbooks instead of eating: neither the firsthand experience nor the sustaining nourishment is provided. In that sense this book is only a springboard; readers are encouraged to experience Native communication and, according to their individual interests, to live in, visit, or create an oral society. This literate introduction is the menu, not the meal.

## ASSUMPTION #2: COMPLEXITY AND SOPHISTICATION AND SUPERIOR

When studying musical composition at the Royal Conservatory, I was warned by an instructor, "How can you possibly wish to bring Indian rhythms and melodies into your work? There is absolutely no comparison between the organizational complexity and brilliant sophistication of Mozart's mathematically precise intervals and the flimsy, repetitive melody of an Indian chant." This is not an uncommon attitude toward Native painting, dance, design, costume, and other art forms.

What if one were to change mindsets? Instead of accusing the lonely Native melody of being barren of any harmony or counterpoint, think of the human voice as part of a larger chorus of animals, wind, and fire. Various tribes were so attuned to listening to the natural world that a seemingly simple melody was the singer's way of *adding* her harmony to the larger natural symphony. Similarly, Native dance may be another element added to the large choreography of wind, animals, stars, seasonal shifts, and dancing shadows.

In her introduction to *The Indians' Book*, Natalie Curtis underscores the importance of hearing Native music in context: "No one who has heard Indian songs in their own environment, under broad skies amid the sweep of wind and grasses, can fail to feel that they are there a note in the nature symphony. Take the Indian from nature, or nature from the Indian, and the Indian's art, if it survives, must undergo the change of supplying from within that which was unconsciously received from without" (Curtis 1987, xxxii). Who is to say that music that harmonizes with life itself is inferior to music with a more intrinsic harmony? Indeed what is advanced, developed, sophisticated, or complex depends largely on framing and context.

In this regard the psychologist Anne Wilson Schaef's observations are instructive. Raised among the Cherokee in the Native way, she noted how important silence, the seeming absence of complex sound, was to Native Americans. "You listened for the *absence* of something," she said, "for when the wind *stopped* or the birds went silent . . . that told you just as much as did sound" (interview, Wilson Schaef, 2/4/91). Who is to say it is more profound to understand progressions of note clusters (chord sequences) than to understand a variety of different silences? Just as the Natives had to learn to listen for a wide range of acoustical subtleties, so we must learn to listen more deeply to appreciate their world.

Harold Innis (1951) and Marshall McLuhan (1964) have suggested that when an individual or society overemphasizes one sense such as seeing, it is more likely to neglect the full range of another sense, such as hearing. Is it not possible that much of the condescension of a "literate" culture toward an "oral" culture, and vice versa, derives from a sensory bias?

## ASSUMPTION #3: COMMUNICATION MAY BE UNDERSTOOD ONLY THROUGH ANALYSIS

As a professor, I have taught communication theory, aesthetics and media criticism, film analysis, and many other courses common to North American universities. Yet my scholarly associate Futa Helu, from the small Native kingdom of Tonga, warns about applying such tools to Polynesian communication: "When theory says 'do X,' we do Y," he cautions. Similarly, Chairman Mao wrote, "To know the apple's taste, you must taste the apple—no amount of theory about the apple's taste will do."

To perceive and analyze only the tip of the iceberg is to fail to understand what is underneath and to ignore the entire process by which water, ice, and icebergs are formed. Similarly, for the Native, communication was merely the uttering or "outering"— the visible tip—of a large but invisible world of meaning. To vivisect or even seek to inspect the invisible was disrespectful of a larger Divine order far more powerful than the human intellect. As Elizabeth Tatar has stated in her dissertation on Hawaiian chant, "All animate and inanimate objects were imbued with some Godly power and were believed to hold a preordained position in the universe. Long, involved rituals and ceremonies were structured to maintain a close rapport between God and man" (Tatar 1982, 13).

In this spirit, most Native expression was not simply "communication," a word that has no equivalent in most ancient and Native languages. The imparting of information was secondary; indeed, in a chant or well-known story the information was already known. Instead, communication simply extended "communion," the natural feeling of oneness with the many kingdoms of nature. Since speaking, singing, dancing, and chanting were all considered sacred, it was the tone, atmosphere, and specific spirit (whether of the Creator or of a specific totem such as Eagle or Coyote) that rendered expression meaningful. To study a song apart from the universal spirit expressing it would be like trying to feel a heartbeat by weighing and measuring an isolated, dead heart.

## A Balanced Approach

Although I am aware of these biases (those discussed above are only a few), I write only partly from the Native perspective. After all, there is nothing inherently wrong with *all* writing, education, Western cultures, or abstraction. So I will seek to borrow tools from *any* cultures that help us better understand the subject. Moreover, people are just as much united by a common humanity as divided by culture. To assume that all our acts are isolated by atomized cultural programming is to deny our common needs and ancestry as persons.

Consequently, Mircea Eliade's *Myths, Rites, and Symbols,* although Western and abstract, may help us better understand events in both Native and industrial societies. Eliade identifies the following common characteristics of rites and rituals: (1) they recover sacred time; (2) they create or gravitate to a sacred setting; (3) they evoke remembrance; (4) they create or re-create new perspectives; and (5) they have an archetype and prototype form. While exceptions always exist, Eliade's descriptions seem to transcend culture and provide an overarching understanding that most oral *and* literate societies could accept. Similarly, his identification of universal communication forms (prayers, death ceremonies, myths, initiations, language, gesture) in *From Primitives to Zen*—seems to help us understand the human tendency to communicate in particular ways in *all* cultures.

Similarly, Owen Barfield's *Speaker's Meaning* helps us understand that some forms of communication, such as language, have more than one function. If, as Barfield indicates, language has two primary functions, *expression,* which aspires toward fullness or sincerity, and *communication,* which aspires toward accuracy, such insights may help us understand not only all cultures, but the differing emphases they give to these functions. Ancient Native communion, for example, seems motivated by the thrust for expression, for outering feelings, ambience, and sacred sensings. Modern industrial societies, by contrast, seem to be characterized more by the second function, given our information explosion, communication revolution, and fact dispensers—from computers to textbooks to journalists.

As we have seen, the external insights of Barfield and Eliade no less than the internal insights of Princess Red Wing St. Cur and Mamoudou Kouyate, provide a multiplicity of perspectives to think about Native expression. Similarly, combining the Native and Western approaches, I will convey *both* my experiences and thought about Native commun(icat)ion.

# CHAPTER TWO

*Stone relief, Mayan ruins, Palenque, Mexico. The Palace, House D, Pier d of the western corridor. Negative #330221; photograph by Berman. Courtesy Department of Library Services, American Museum of Natural History.*

# Early Communication

I n Western civilization, human "communication" is seen as a skill that has either evolved or devolved with humanity. Scientific theorists believe that humans have evolved from lower life forms and note how our species has developed from speaking mere grunts and groans to using sophisticated satellites and interacting computers. We have evolved from a species with tiny brains to one that not only *has* much larger brains but can *produce* larger artificial brains (computers) as well as eyes (telescopes), ears (antennae), and tongues (transmitters).

Many religious people believe that humans have "fallen" from some more perfect state and claim that we have *devolved*. That is, we have lost our higher powers of long-distance communication—communion with all animals and understanding the rhythms of nature. However proud we are of the tinker toys of modern technology, they argue, we have had to develop numerous specialists—marriage counselors, lawyers, consultants, family therapists, psychiatrists, and so on—to assist us to talk with and understand each other and ourselves. We no longer truly communicate.

Authentic Native Peoples empathize more with this latter view. While many tribal people have, of necessity, become Westernized and use mass media, they have usually preferred silence to electronic noise, live ceremony to taped drama, slow-paced activity to accelerated voices (such as in ads and disc jockey monologues), and natural encounters with their neighbors to imported, edited, violent, sexy images of unknown and distant peoples.

"Aboriginals" have often resented the idea that they should look like or be like images used in advertising, especially the idea that they should purchase endless useless products to imitate an artificial lifestyle. In short they have been forced to devolve into a more artificial, commercial, and superficial type of communication.

## Literate Societies

Two of the communication practices that settlers brought to Native cultures were formal rules and evolving tools. Most European expansion to Africa, Australia, and the Americas was by *Christian* colonists whose inherited rules were not only those of the state, such as against seditious language but those of the Church, such as the Ten Commandments: "Thou shalt not bear false witness against thy neighbor" (Exod. 20:16); "Thou shalt not make unto thee any graven image" (Exod. 20:4); "Thou shalt not take the name of the Lord thy God in Vain" (Exod. 20:7). What was most confusing to many Natives was that the missionary sought to instill these rules among converts while the soldier and settler abandoned the rules by lying, swearing, and "bearing false witness" against their (Native) neighbors.

A multicultural heritage supported the Christian moral rules brought by settlers. Western communication "ethics" may be traced as far back as Hammurabi (ca. 1925 B.C.) whose legal code spelled out specific undesirable modes of communication: "If a seignior accuses (another) seignior and brings a charge of murder against him, but cannot prove it, his accuser shall be put to death" (cited in Pritchard 1958, 139). Other penalties, such as those for false accusation of sorcery or adultery, were equally serious. Implicit within Hammurabi's code was an ethic favoring truth-telling that set the precedent for Western libel law (Pritchard 1958, 139–171).

Many rules of the Hebrews, as recorded in the Torah, were not significantly different. In Deuteronomy (5:20) it had been written, "Neither shalt thou bear false witness against thy neighbor," and in Exodus (23:1), "Thou shalt not raise a false report: put not thine hand with the wicked to be an unrighteous witness."

Such rulemaking was commonplace among colonial societies. When Islamic conquerors sought to convert Native Peoples much later, the communication rules of the Koran were brought forth: "Those who blaspheme his name shall assuredly be recompensed" (193) and "woe unto every backbiter, slanderer" (349). In "The Loosed Ones" within the Koran, or its fifty lines of poetry, ten lines iterate "woe that day unto those who cry lies" (318).

Nothing about this outlook would have surprised the ancient Egyptians. After death their hearts were symbolically weighed on one side of a balance scale against the Goddess Ma'at's feather of Truth (Demott 2/10/91). Truth was the prime value, and lying was forbidden by Pharaonic law. A similar emphasis on truth informed the Christian New Testament scriptures (e.g., John 17:17, "Sanctify them in the truth; Thy word is truth"; John 18:37, "Everyone that is of the truth heareth my voice.")

"Western" civilization, which drew on Babylonian, Egyptian, Greek, Roman, Hebrew, Christian, and other traditions, imported this legacy of codified communication concepts. Eventually the legacy would be categorized by the West as obscenity, libel, profanity, plagiarism, pornography, slander, blasphemy, and other ideas often unfamiliar to tribal peoples. Herbert Muller (1961, 59–61) suggests that even the seemingly modern concept "freedom of speech" has antecedents in civilizations as ancient as the early Egyptians' and that a word meaning "freedom" was introduced in the twenty-fourth century B.C. by King Urukagina of Lagos (page 37). Yet colonists fighting for a "free press" would find little empathy among Natives untrained in print technology; nor would their press be free to most tribal peoples.

The "white man" was proud of communication tools such as the printing press and the book, which demonstrated "superior" intellect, learning, and advanced abstraction. Eventually Europeans would also introduce cameras, telegraph lines, electricity, postal communication, and long-distance signaling systems in the "taming" of the "territories." Western civilization seemed proud of these technologies that had evolved from earlier tools such as clay tablets, parchment, and papyrus. Evolving technologies also served as a means of control. The economic historian Harold Innis has noted that those who owned communication implements could develop "monopolies of knowledge" unavailable to their rivals or victims (see Innis, 1951 and 1952). For example, a book about how to make guns and gunpowder is a valued "monopoly of knowledge" to the literate but of no value to the nonliterate. Similarly, a printing press can produce identical copies of a detailed map for dozens of army battalions scattered across hundreds of miles. On unknown territory their opponents may become more easily confused, lost, isolated, divided, and conquered without the unifying maps. Writing and replication made possible the notion of "treaties" and "contracts," the primary documents of control.

Innis further noted that each communication seemed to change the social structure into which it was introduced. Marshall McLuhan later simplified this idea: "The medium is the message." Each medium—print, the telephone, radio, television— has left its mark on oral societies.

European colonists had inherited a knowledge of imperial communications from their many ancestors. As Toynbee noted, in ancient societies

*The postmen . . . were very often policemen. A public postal service seems to have been part of the machinery of the government of the Empire of Sumer and Akked in the third millennium B. C. In the Archaemenian Empire . . . two thousand years later the imperial communications system (was) maintaining the central government's control over the provinces (and) reappears in the administration of the Roman Empire and of the Arab caliphate." (Toynbee 87)*

As postal and telegraph systems were established in wilderness areas, uniform messages could be disbursed throughout. Settlers could magnify their power by, for example, requesting more supplies, tools, books, weapons, or soldiers. News of neighboring attacks and epidemics would be more accurately transmitted. Centralized orders—to attack, mobilize, relocate, or coordinate maneuvers—could be more precisely orchestrated.

On the larger level, a distant language, culture, and structured consciousness could be superimposed on Natives by mailing and transporting thoughts. For example, the Pony Express could broadcast widely the order that those who did not obey the U.S. Cavalry could be shot on command. And in parts of Africa, the warning that anyone who did not learn English would be enslaved could be uniformly distributed. Around the world, those who did learn English were often taught first how to read the Bible. Ultimately, writing and print propagated and proselytized for a foreign order.

## Oral Societies

*Original communication implied a state of innocence in which nothing is hidden nor imposed. [It was] a simple and straightforward affair. Such communication would engage the entire psycho-spiritual mechanism. . . . Indeed our form of communication is very foreign to surviving tribes. (Interview, Heinberg 8/15/90)*

Rather than depend on elaborate rules and evolving tools, early Native communication was probably characterized by silent simplicity and a profound communion with the sacred or supernatural. In mythologies (histories of Native Peoples), there are repetitive, if unproven, references to what might now be called telepathy, a universal and inaudible language spoken by animals and people. Indeed part of the early fascination some Europeans had for some Natives pertained to a seeming instinctual understanding Indigenous People had for animals, plants, and weather patterns. It was as if all these life forms somehow engaged in transparent telecommunication.

Virtually all Native societies existed prior to their encounters with Europeans. For example, archaeologists have dated (via carbon-14 tests) artifacts from the Pinson Mounds, Native ceremonial and burial sites of western Tennessee, at thirteen hundred years earlier than white settlement. More significant, "lost" peoples, such as the "red paint" people of Ballybrack, Labrador, have been dated to 7500 B.C. Modified pyramids and earth domes found throughout the world predate colonial settlements by one, two, or even several millennia. Indeed, as best we understand "cavemen," they were probably tribal people.

Despite the mounting archaeological discoveries of traces of ancient tribal peoples, there is little concrete "evidence" for most of their communication practices. By definition, oral societies retained and refined memories by oral and mnemonic means, rather than through storage systems such as scrolls and tablets. One impressive exception is cave painting, such as those found in Altamira, Spain, which were probably used as backdrops for religious ceremonies.

If the secular Western world communicated its official past through type and "history," the Native world, like the religious sector of Western society, preferred myth and mystery. Typically, Native myths involved some means of storytelling to (1) provide a sacred and entertaining drama for the tribe, its men, or its women; (2) educate young people, boys, or girls; (3) directly or indirectly resolve tribal issue or tensions; (4) experience the artistry of the storyteller; (5) evoke or emphasize awe, mystery, or connection with Divine forces; (6) sustain a continuity of cultural bonding and heritage across the generations; (7) experience catharsis, healing, magic, or (super)natural spirits.

Hence the myth held a central position in collective internal communication. Elsewhere Claude Lévi-Strauss, Mircea Eliade, Joseph Campbell, and others have elaborated the structure and function of myth (see References).

Within the important commentary *Memories and Visions of Paradise* (1989), Richard Heinberg has synthesized specific myths which depict the original state of humanity. These tend to imply that human communication, like humanity, has *devolved* from a higher state. For example, Heinberg notes,

> *Many traditions say that the first human beings spoke a single language. . . . [I]n the myths of the Chins and the Twyan of Indochina, all people could understand one another's speech until the collapse of a tower or ladder built in an attempt to reach Heaven. The Mayans likewise say that the First People "had but a single language." Some traditions go further,*

*suggesting that in Paradise humanity was telepathic; the Hopi, for example, say that the First People "felt as one and understood one another without talking." (1989, 65)*

Moreover, he states that such a universal language "seems to have extended to the animal kingdom as well."

Despite the challenge of fully visualizing this unproven utopian condition, it is important to "walk a mile in their moccasins." For Native peoples, myth was not merely suggestive or symbolic; what *we* call myth was for them real. Even if it is difficult to accept the *literal* truth of these or other myths, it is important to acknowledge their value as symbol or metaphor and to honor the fact that many cultures view myth as others view history. Thus many Indigenous People fully believed in a previous state of elevated expression described in creation songs, myths, and rituals.

Some ancient higher powers of communication were indicated or implied in oral literature, such as the following:

1. **Creation via communication.** Australian Aboriginals and American Navajos thought that originally Beings and objects could be "sung into existence." A variety of cultures indicate that physical entities were chanted, thought, or sung into being.
2. **Communication with Divinity.** Often this was depicted as a rainbow or ladder of rope (rather than words) between God(s) and humans. Reportedly, the Mayans (and many others) "spoke the same language as the Gods and understood the Gods perfectly" (Heinberg 1989, 69–70).
3. **The potency of silence.** Numerous references indicate that the universe came from silence or a void. Creation, vision (as in the vision quest), and important words were preceded by silence. In more recent centuries the Iroquois reportedly sat in silence for days, until the interpersonal atmosphere and climate for communication was clear and harmonious.

4. **A universal, intuitive language** (discussed above).

5. **Physical luminosity.** Tibetan, Kalmach, and Siberian lore indicate that human flesh once gave off visible light (Heinberg 1989, 68). In other stories, humans, like Gods, used natural (not artificial) light to communicate.

6. **Unified vibration.** An entire group, gathering, or city of Native People may have sung, spoken, or chanted simultaneously, creating a potent, unified, pulse of sound.

7. **Inherent truthfulness.** "A time before the first lie" (before "forked tongue") is implicit in most Creation stories. In the pre-Chinese original Age of Harmony, for example, there was no clear distinction between self and others. Thus to lie to the other was to lie to one's self. It was impossible to lie effectively until the age when the individual felt inwardly divided or separate from society. Hindu prehistory implies a first age of "truth-*speaking.*" The second age is of "truth-*seeking,*" the third of "truth-*declining,*" and the fourth (present day) of "very little truth remaining."

8. **Direct Commands.** Hollywood has melodramatically depicted Native cultures in which empowered words cast spells, work voodoo, and effect magical healings. While most of these scenarios are sensationalized, Indigenous myths indicate far grander edicts were issued by early God-beings, some of which created mountains, species, or the sun. For example, in the Maori (New Zealand people) creation myth, a "direct command" is depicted thus: There was no glimmer of dawn, no clearness, no light. And he (a Maori God) began by saying these words: "Darkness, Become a Light-Possessing Darkness!" And at once light appeared (Heinberg 1989, 24).

For Indigenous People it was easy to envision an earlier period in which Godlike ancestors, giant Animal spirits, or powerful plants gave emphatic orders. Everything surrounding them—a lake shaped like a giant footprint, a mountain resembling a reclining coyote, moving stars (comets), lightning bolts from the invisible—suggested natural Sources and unseen Forces at work throughout the universe. When the wind moved from tree to tree in the forest, it was easy to picture Windwalker, a spirit that moved freely throughout the woods. Nor was there anything irrational in assuming that if the Sun and Rain could create crops and forests from tiny seeds, they could create humanity and wildlife as well.

For many Aboriginal People "communication" was a releasing of a stored power. Speaking, singing, shouting, gesturing, staring, and other forms of expression allowed *potential* energy to become *kinetic* energy. Depending on the occasion, communication could be seen as a transforming, transferring, unleashing, or sharing of power, whether destructive or creative.

For example, the Polynesian peoples believed in *mana*, which Rubellite Johnson (interview, 1/14/91) calls "a psychodynamic power," a power closely associated with thought or consciousness. Two of the most important characteristics of mana are that it "manifests the power of the Gods in the human world" and it is "always linked to organic generativity and thus to all forces of growth and vitality." When Kahunas (Polynesian spiritual leaders) transform invisible man into specific ritual activities, the invisible power of the Gods is transmuted into visible results such as changing weather, healing, a fuller harvest, or an energized ceremony.

Often before a Native leader spoke to white immigrants, his silence was not only a sign of respect but also a "gathering of the energies" or a "summoning of mana" prior to utterance. While mana and the related notion *tabu* (forbidden) was primarily Polynesian, many other Native societies had a similar sense that words were simply an utterance (or outering) of a stored charge.

Thus there were two contexts of Native communication to which the European emissary was blind and deaf: first, tribal myths tied Native communication to a hidden but lapsed epoch of perfect and supraliminal communication; second, words and gestures came from a more immediate Divine interior transformer. *Mana*, or its next of kin, provided a charged carrier wave, for which words were mere cargo.

## Summary: Literate versus Oral

As the European settler imported moral rules and printing tools, colonial outposts depended on *externally* imposed methods of communication. Native expression, conversely, relied more on *internal* transmission characterized by intuition, silent communion, memorized myth, and invisible power storage. *External* communications, whether through animal dances or sweat lodge ceremonies, were merely the means of making manifest voltage silently generated within.

In this context one better understands why chiefs and generals misunderstood each other. For the general, the peace treaty was a specific *tool* by which *rules* might be established. For the chief, paper had little meaning, nor did *ownership*—since all land was owned by the Great Spirit. It was the *tone* of dialogue, the *quality* of communion, the *atmosphere* of trust, the *sharing* of lands, the generation of *accord* that mattered most to the chief in the early "peace" ceremonies.

An emphasis on tools (such as treaties) and inflexible rules (the terms of agreement) seemed unnatural and forbidding to oral societies, just as fences (which represent tools as well as the imposition of rules) seem imprisoning to many contemporary Natives. There was no mythos, no mystery, and no mana in such linear, literate, and legalistic arrangements.

Moreover, there was no adherence to legal documents by their creators. Like Hammurabi's code, the Ten Commandments, and many European laws, treaties seemed made to be broken. In the United States, for example, *every* treaty between Natives and the U.S. government was violated. The Indian, whose sacred covenant with others was always to be honored and who had a mythic memory of "a time before lying," was saddened and shocked by the faked accord, by the forked tongue.

## BEYOND HISTORY: NATIVE ORIGINS

How one views authentic Aboriginal communications depends on how one views Native origins. I consider below both the Western (evolutionary) and Native (devolutionary) accounts of Native origins and migration.

Most Native Peoples are purported to have migrated to their present homes from other continents or islands. Indigenous western Canadians and Americans presumably crossed the Bering Strait from Asia and descended into warmer climates. Presumably, native Hawaiians were formerly Polynesian islanders who sailed east on wooden boats. Reportedly, Indigenous Africans and Australians were also "settlers" from a distant place and past. Often such theories of migration are based on evidence that peoples in different locations have similar customs, languages, or physical features. Indeed some specific forms of Native communication— drumming, group chanting, creation storytelling, harvest dancing—persist across oceans and deserts. Some of the linguistic and ceremonial patterns of the coastal Salish People of British Columbia, for example, seem derivative of their East Asian counterparts.

If one believes the evolutionary accounting of history, it is easy to assume that migration was a response to the ongoing process of natural selection. In such a view survival was contingent on

*An elephant hunt. Native mural decorations upon an Azando hut. Bwendi's place near the Aka River, near Faradje, former Belgian Congo. Negative #221253; photograph by Herbert Lang, Oct. 1911. Courtesy Department of Library Services, American Museum of Natural History.*

finding an improved environment for breeding and feeding, for maintaining and advancing one's species. Immigrants (who were not yet "natives") traveled in search of more advantageous climates, hunting, fishing, or farming. Alternatively, as emigrants they may have been distancing themselves from rivals, predators, droughts, or other adverse conditions.

Similarly, from the evolutionary perspective, it would be argued that Native communication arose to meet local environmental needs. Migration into mountain and plateau areas would favor the creation of communication systems like smoke signals, which could be seen afar and above. In contrast, the plains of Africa or America might favor *drumming*, which could be heard for great distances, so long as there were no intervening mountains.

An evolutionist might argue that animal species survived which developed competitive communication systems. For example, rabbits with eyes at the *sides* of their heads could see better and evade predators more easily than rabbits with eyes at the front of their heads. Even so, the evolutionist would argue that those tribes which adapted their communication to the environment, so as to compete favorably with predators and rivals, were more likely to survive.

Native Peoples account for their origins in much different ways, without Darwinian principles and migration studies. Rather than a horizontal migration, across the earth's surface, Native legends often speak of a *vertical* movement into their present homeland. Such movement takes a variety of forms—from or through the heavens, through a hole in the earth or the clouds, climbing up or down from one plane or earth to another, descending as birds or (the offsprings of) Gods, falling, and climbing down ladders.

Often such legends imply a change of state during the birth of humanity, such as from God to (wo)man, from Divine animal to (hu)man, from the heavens (whether Sun, Moon, Stars, Sky, or whatever) to human or similar transformation. From this standpoint, ancient communication practices have *developed* or *devolved* into mere remnant or residual traditions that echo a bygone era. Rather than being an adaptation to the local environment, a Native ceremony is more like a faded photograph or a dimly remembered event, more changed by time and state of mind than by relocation and natural selection.

Since the evolutionary interpretation of natural history is already well described in Western science, I will give attention here to views that might account for the Native notion of *devolution,* beyond our normal views of "history" and "science." If we view Native ceremonies as remnants of a higher legacy, of more advanced "tribes" who preceded them, we may view their communication with greater respect and understanding.

Conversely, the outsider's evolutionist frame of reference leads to the condescending perspective of "savages" who, just one step above the apes, evolved a slightly higher order of communication than the primates. According to that view, the grunts and groans of gorillas became a "primitive" monosyllabic vocabulary ("How, "heap big rock," "bwana") which portrayed tribal people as an inferior subspecies.

In the oral literature of most Indigenous People is the record of a great flood, rain, or catastrophe. Whatever the nature of that upheaval, it was reportedly necessary for groups to disperse, flee, or escape, rather than simply migrate. If the biblical accounting of a tower of Babel and Noah's ark metaphorically tell similar stories, a universal prehistory may be postulated, based on the "postdiluvian" (oral) literature of virtually all cultures. A higher civilization was all but erased by traumatic upheavals (whether flood, famine, near-collisions with celestial bodies, glaciers, or earthquakes) and survivors sought any place of refuge.

One undocumented account of such an upheaval was by Lloyd Meeker, Sr., who stated that Native Peoples as distant as Mexico, the Himalayas, Honduras, and South America had escaped the submergence of Lemuria, a legendary lost continent inundated by the Pacific Ocean. He noted that the higher elevations of Lemuria still remain unsubmerged as South Sea island groups. The Easter Islands still contain "solid stones which simply could not have been quarried by the best engineers today" (Meeker, *Loveland Fireside Chats* 1944, 2). Meeker felt that most of the ancient continent sank, as if in response to a monumental earthquake, but remnants, such as the "solid stones," may still be found in the remaining islands.

Using the name "Mu" as a shortened form of "Lemuria," James Churchward popularized the controversial "lost continent" perspective in a series of books published in the 1930s. Basing his writings on interpretations of the *Naacal* tablets in India and on interpretations of stone tablets in Mexico, Churchward decided that he had deciphered inspired symbolic writing from a refined (pre-)civilization. Like Heinberg fifty years later, Churchward demonstrated parallels among Polynesian, Hindu, Laotian, and other creation myths (Churchward 1959, 42). He suspected that ancient Native communication, such as among cliff dwellers in North America and the Yucatán people, alluded to Mu and deciphered their most ancient symbols accordingly (220–270).

Eventually Churchward became so fascinated with the residual symbols of early Native People that he dedicated entire books to explaining the sacred forces and symbols of Mu. Such symbols, he asserted, transferred into (now) "native" societies not only an encoding of the past (memory of lost ancestors and heritage) but maintained an ongoing vertical connection with "Deity." While the memory of what these symbols represented faded, mutations of previous ceremonies and songs survived Mu with a variety of tribal and geographic "accents" spread throughout the world.

While it is impossible to prove or disprove the often unscholarly claims of Churchward, his work points to a retranslation of Native "art." The missionary's tendency was to see simple Native symbols and cave pictures as "primitive," like a child's drawings, given their absence of perspective, shadings, and verisimilitude. But who is to say to what these so-called elementary markings and figures refer? If Churchward's evidence seems all too neatly organized to defy the untidiness of reality, he nevertheless posed a profitable line of questioning: Why do similar, even identical, ancient markings appear in remote parts of the world? What overlap or uniformity of communication existed prior to European colonization? What does it mean?

Scholars are justifiably skeptical of Churchward's "evidence." No one living has seen the Naacal tablets. Nevertheless, the larger literature on lost continents that spreads to Plato and modern theorists and on overarching symbols of communication cannot be easily dismissed.

## FREUD'S, JUNG'S, AND VELIKOVSKY'S CONTROVERSIAL VIEWS

The most thorough examination of a common cataclysmic prehistory was researched by Immanuel Velikovsky in a series of books published between 1950 and 1982. Seeking on the one hand to understand six hundred-year discrepancies between Egyptian and Israeli records (*Ages in Chaos*, 1952) and on the other to integrate widespread ancient accounts of celestial and terrestrial traumas (*Worlds in Collision*, 1950) Velikovsky rewrote history in a manner that shook the orthodox academic community.

Claiming that major cataclysms occurred 2,700 and 3,500 years ago, and correlating these with ancient records, Velikovsky

*Pictograph painted on the rocky walls of a canyon in Cimarron County, Oklahoma. Some similar pictographs are thought to portray the histories of tribes that lived here before the coming of the Europeans. Photograph © by Marcia Keegan.*

pressed much farther than others by seeking the *causes* of human ignorance of such upheavals. As a trained psychoanalyst, Velikovsky argued that humanity acts like an amnesia victim seeking to repress a traumatic experience. In *Mankind in Amnesia* (1982), he fully developed his case, first noting how amnesia is characterized in the individual:

> *A victim of amnesia may live adjacent to neighbors who are completely unaware of his plight. He may be employed, he may be married, he may behave on the surface like anybody else. But he has forgotten everything before a certain date. . . .*
>
> *Amnesia need not affect all memory; it may affect only certain areas of the past. Such cases are very numerous and rarely is a neurotic personality free from some area of oblivion; characteristically, the oblivion erases the most painful or terrorizing reminiscences. (p. 9)*

Velikovsky argued that humanity conveniently remembered its "progress" after "devolution" but not the disturbing catastrophes it had suffered.

On this point, Velikovsky was not a maverick. Sigmund Freud, for example, had noted in his later writing that humanity at large could act just like a mentally disturbed individual:

> *If we consider mankind as a whole and substitute it for a single individual, we discover that it too has developed delusions which are inaccessible to logical criticism and which contradict reality. If, in spite of this, they (the delusions) are able to exert an extraordinary power over men, investigation leads us to the same explanation as in the case of the single individual. They owe their power to the element of historical truth which they have brought up from the repression of the forgotten and primeval past. (Freud 1978, vol. 3, 269)*

To some degree Freud's notion of a collectively psychotic humanity is affirmed by Carl Jung's vision of "the collective unconscious," delineated in 1934:

> *A more or less superficial layer of the unconscious is undoubtedly personal. I call it the* personal unconscious. *But this personal unconscious rests upon a deeper layer, which does not derive from personal experience and is not a personal acquisition but is inborn. This deeper layer I call the* collective unconscious. . . . *It is, in other words, identical in all men and thus constitutes a common psychic substrate of a suprapersonal nature which is present in every one of us. (Jung 1934, 6–7)*

For Jung, humanity's race memory flows through individuals over centuries as an ocean wave flows through water molecules. In other words, "germ cells . . . carry life for untold generations, using the individual organism as their carrier" (Jung cited in Velikovsky 1982, 29).

As Velikovsky saw it, humanity is unaware of both its (Jungian) collective memory and its (Velikovskian) collective amnesia. Similarly, a patient with scotoma is unaware of blind spots. In ophthalmology, scotoma is a partial or insular blindness. A certain segment of the field of vision "does not register on the retina because of some defect, like detachment of the retina or a clot of blood beneath it. Psychological scotoma is an inability to observe certain phenomena or to recognize certain situations though they are obvious to other persons" (Velikovsky 1982, 10).

The image of a humankind with amnesia is not entirely original to Velikovsky. Plato warned that the Lethe, River of Forgetfulness, had erased our awareness of the Ideas, an absolute knowledge of universal principals. In Hinduism, Buddhism, and Gnosticism, "sin" is forgetting one's true self (Heinberg 1989, 98).

Indeed many religions and philosophies call for some level of "awakening," as from amnesia or hypnosis, to a different identity or perspective.

Without seeking to prove or disprove these psychologists, one may sense a provocative spirit at work in their collective inquiry. A shared forgetfulness and a shared memory suggest a more profound approach to examining Native communication. What if Native ceremonies carry seeds of memory of a common past? Could tribal communications convey, not so much an "evolved aboriginal slime," as the slower rhythms and sacred atmosphere derived from an earlier, refined state? What if Native rituals cannot be understood at face value? Does their "meaning" tie us to a greater universal order or previous mode of communication? Are tribal and literate societies doomed to cultural apartheid? Or are we both different dialects of a lost language?

Even in the notion of evolving tools, it seems valuable to be open-minded. What if, once again, as some Native societies teach, our mass media have "devolved" from higher technologies? Peter Tompkins's examination of the Great Pyramid of Giza raises such questions:

> *An engineer and former professor of radio, L. Turenae, maintains that all sorts of different forms—being combinations of different frequencies—act as different types of resonators . . . [such] that the Pyramid might be some sort of gigantic lens which is able to focus an unknown energy simply by means of its shape. Even the coffer in the King's Chamber has been considered such a device by Worth Smith, who points out that the cubic capacity of the coffer is exactly the same as that of the Biblical Arc of the Covenant. (Tompkins 1971, 278)*

There is far more to read of the pyramids' inexplicable mathematical, astronomical, and magnetic potency (as in Tompkins' *Secrets of the Great Pyramids*) and of the geophysical, systemic "magic" of Stonehenge (as in Hawkins' *Stonehenge Decoded*). What is significant is that these and other ancient ruins seemed designed for communicating, in an all but supernatural manner, such stunning knowledge as the earth's distance from the sun, its circumference, exact time-keeping, and important ratios. Some theorists have even conjectured that another level of communication may well have been involved, communication that, in Native terms, would have been on behalf of, in communion with, or directly from the Gods.

If a "higher intelligence" once communicated through human beings or their technologies, who is to argue this "higher" residue is less present among Indigenous societies than among the European literati? After all, Mayan and Aztec societies, deemed "Native" but hardly uncivilized, were considered architecturally and technically advanced by the Spaniards who "discovered" them. Were not such societies also among the literati?

The South American Cogi of the past millennia had elaborate maps, teachings, and temples born of a fascinating acumen. Indeed the Cogi seem to have resisted outside encroachment (missionaries did not obtain a single convert; teachers did not win one student to writing), not because they would become civilized, but rather, given their own values, because they would become uncivilized, that is, because they would defile their own internal order. What inspired and preceded these "Native" societies?

## A PRECAUTION AGAINST STEREOTYPE

In taking seriously the Native notion that humans came from a higher ancestry, one may easily substitute a new stereotype—

the saintly, superhuman Native—for the old one—the heathen savage. To do so would be to ignore evidence of ritual killing, cannibalism, tribal wars, and human sacrifice in both ancient and modern tribes. However, if the "higher" ancestry view is taken, such "barbarian" practices may nevertheless be better understood. As Grace Van Duzen notes, survivors of cataclysms would have faced extreme heat, cold, and starvation and pending extinction (interview 8/29/90). Cannibalism might well have been the only alternative to starvation after such upheavals. What are now viewed as "pagan" or "heathen" atrocities, such as human sacrifice, may have also occurred during an extreme stage of devolution, as if to appease angry Gods who had created such an uproar.

Most, if not all, contemplation of any stages of devolution, is strictly speculative from a Western, modern standpoint. Thus Van Duzen cautions against substituting myths for truth, or literal interpretations of ancient texts for wisdom. She further cautions against assuming that "race memory" from a lost continent or Motherland, such as Lemuria, Atlantis, Eden, or "the Happy Hunting Ground," is accurate. After all, if we inaccurately remember what happened fifteen minutes ago, why should race memory perfectly preserve what transpired fifteen *millennia* ago?

What is important is not establishing new and exacting theories of Native origin but being open to considering various accounts and perspectives. Native ceremony may have evolved in adaptation to its environment. But it may just as well carry "memory," "residue," "fragments" of an era of highly refined communication. Whether or not Freud, Jung, Velikovsky, Meeker, and even Churchward are accurate, their work prods us to consider that current theories about Indigenous origins and human memory may well be shallow, even dogmatic. What alternative explanations account for overlapping tribal communication practices worldwide? Is it possible that we have "forgotten" parts of our past? Were Indigenous Peoples once more united? Regal? Empowered? "Evolved?" If so, when the forms of Native communication are considered in the next chapter, it will be vital to consider that their meaning and heritage may be greater than appears on the surface.

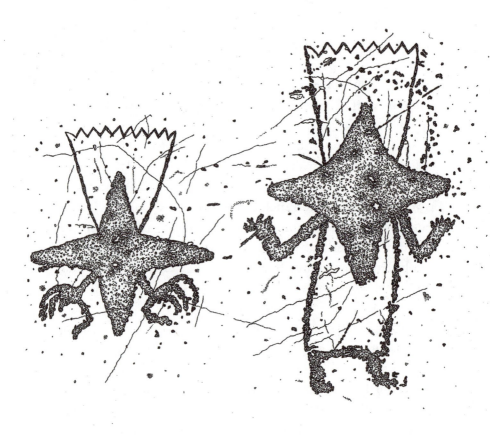

*Anasazi "star beings" from petroglyph site near Albuquerque, New Mexico. Drawing © by Sabra Moore.*

# CHAPTER THREE

*Old Kuba mask from Central Zaire. Courtesy of Judy Fein. Photograph © by Marcia Keegan.*

## Indigenous Forms
## of Communication

There may be more *forms* of Indigenous communication than groups of people. In some groups, each person has her own song. Tales are told that in some vanished tribes, each person had his own unique instrument. After reading thousands of books and articles about hundreds of tribes, I am aware of no groups without unique modes of communication—crafts, chants, dialect, telepathy, hand signals, among dozens of others.

Later in this chapter I will list many of these forms. A danger of such a listing is that each form appears to be a separate and isolated artifact, sterilized for museum display. From a Native perspective, however, no form of expression can be meaningfully separated from its purpose or its sacred place, or from Spirit(s), or from the perceptions and feelings of the communicator. So I will begin with these larger contexts, rather than the forms.

### Purpose and Philosophy

As a child Becca Johnson had known Chief Dan George. Forty years later she could still remember his impact as an unusual communicator: "He never spoke unless he had something to say. He honored the silences which make us (non-Natives)

uncomfortable . . . when he did speak, it was something worthwhile and carried weight. . . . There was great wisdom" (interview
Becca Johnson 5/5/91). Unlike Becca's other Canadian friends,
Chief Dan George never spoke without a reason. So to analyze his
grammar, or content, or even style would be to miss the most
important and most frequent part of his communication, his
silences. What was more important than George's words was that
such words were born only of purpose. He had a purpose for
silence, and a purpose for speaking.

Similarly, Anne Wilson Schaef, the American psychologist,
remembered profound silences when she was raised among
Cherokees. Natives listened for the absence of sound, such as
when the wind stopped or the animals became quiet. Silence was
not the absence of sound, nor was it a form; it was a seamless
external and internal presence with many possible purposes:
expressing respect, reverence, outer listening, inner listening,
communion with nature, perceiving shifts in weather, worship.
Sometimes the purpose for silence was more mysterious and thus
difficult to articulate.

In some tribes it was expected that one would consider how
long one wished to speak and then be silent for that length of time
before speaking, so as to give proper thought and tone to what
would be said. In such cases, the philosophy of communication
indicated that what was expressed needed to be worthy of the
listener and of the length of time allotted for speech. Hence the
*form* of communication grew from a larger context—silence—and
reflected a specific philosophy and purpose.

### SPIRITS

In her dissertation on Hawaiian chant, Elizabeth Tatar refuses to
study the *form* of chant in a vacuum: both manu and kapu (invisible spiritual forces) are "very important in the composition

and performance of chant in Hawaii" (Tatar 1982, 16); "long involved rituals and ceremonies were structured to maintain a close rapport between God and man" (13). Art was a vehicle for intercourse with the Divine and could not be extracted into mere techniques.

Indeed Native art does not seem to recognize the Western concept of art for art's sake. Art may only exist for the sake of something *other* than its own form or content. For example, the sand paintings of the Navajo "provide a conduit for gods to enter bodies of those seeking cures" (Hoffman 1974, 67); the *purpose* of the paintings is to assist with healing. Similarly, Native American dancing often provides a path whereby Spirits, such as animal guardian Spirits, ancestors, or all living beings, may enter into the bodies and souls of the dancers (Hoffman 1974, 37).

In this light, accuracy is sometimes more important than, and sometimes identical to, aesthetics. One Navajo elder stated, "Our people have always described a singer as 'good' rather than as 'beautiful' in describing his performance." It seemed far more important to the elder that the song be sung by one who would faithfully remember each part of it, who would actually provide an accurate conduit for the gods to enter the earth, than that the singer have a talented or trained voice.

Again a philosophy of service is suggested: the song and dance serve a higher order. Indeed, if the sounds or signs are not accurately conveyed, the entire spiritual experience could be impotent or even destructive. If there is a Western equivalent, it is the tradition that art need be "inspired," as by Plato's Muses, rather than merely meet Aristotle's standards requiring a symmetrical structure constructed of perfect parts.

The Native philosophy of service to a higher order is articulated by N. Scott Momaday in his description of the experience of the Native singer:

*The singer stands at the center of sound, of motion, of life. Nothing within the whole sphere of being is inaccessible to him or lost upon him. At least we have the sense that this is so and so does he. His song if full of reverence and wonder, and delight and of confidence as well. (1976, 294)*

*In short, art cannot exist on its own—it extends a pre-existing order. This order, or energy, is not the singer's own device, but a current into which he enters and is sustained in his spirit. He believes that language is intrinsically powerful, that it is yet another and indeed indispensable dimension of the house in which he dwells. It is, moreover, the dimension in which his existence is most fully accomplished. He does not create language, but is himself created within it. (1976, 297)*

This "Native American" notion would be well understood by Hawaiian peoples. As Elizabeth Kuualoha explains, "The Hawaiian *language* is a spiritual experience. It gives Life and seems connected to something far grander than just the human beings who speak it" (interview 2/1/91). In speaking of a greater Hawaiian *rhythm,* she suggests that nature, music, and indigenous actions all seem interpenetrated by it.

It is equally impossible to separate communication forms from the social and educational activity of the tribe: Kuualoha notes that there was once a unique chant to accompany each craft or work party. All skills and group history were taught in chant format. (The English alphabet chant—"a, b, c, d, e, f, g," etc., sung by first-graders, is an interesting parallel in *letter,* if not in *spirit.*)

## Enhanced Perception and Feelings

Another context in which Indigenous communication is embedded takes on, by Western appraisal, a "supernatural" quality. For example, like "Superman" in Western mythology, the "superscout" of tribal legends is reported to have extraordinary sensory powers, near X-ray vision, long-distance smell, and full-spectrum hearing. In many cases these powers might be viewed as enhanced, multilevel perception, as Tom Brown's character Stalking Wolf in *The Vision* demonstrates:

> *Stalking Wolf pushed himself to observe at all levels, not only on the physical level but also on a deeper, more encompassing, spiritual level. Eventually his skills transcended the mere senses, and he began to reach beyond to the force of life itself. The confluence of spiritual sensing and spiritual awareness was eventually so complete that when asked how he knew something was moving in the distance, he was often at a loss to explain. Complete awareness became for him a state of being. It was said of him that if a feather dropped from a bird several miles away, Grandfather (Stalking Wolf) would know about it. . . . [N]othing happened that he could not feel. (Brown 1988, 17)*

From a distance, there seems to be nothing dramatic about these forms of communication: no technologies are involved in the seemingly subtle, if not invisible, realms of perception that often involve only one person. Yet these were the forms of communication that were invaluable for successful cooperation with nature and, in some cases, for survival. Here is how Brown describes the communication mode of the Apache hunter:

> *Absolute proficiency of these skills—the ability to move, silent and unseen, across landscapes with little cover, the ability to*

*read tracks quickly and accurately, and an uncanny ability to observe all things at a glance—were essential to a scout. Tracking, stalking, and awareness are never separated but rather viewed as a whole, a sort of continuum in which one is dependent on the others for absolute precision and perfection. These skills, coupled with the ability to survive, made of the scout a shadowy ghost, mystical and shrouded in an air of secrecy and legend, much like the ancient ninjas. (Brown 1988, 16)*

It seems fair to suggest that this perception extends beyond what might be called "enhanced" use of the senses to include more intuitive and subconscious "senses." That is, many diverse Native communication skills extend to what the West, for lack of a better term, has lumped under the category "ESP," or extra-sensory perception. An engaging recent example is narrated by Hawaiian scholar Rubellite Johnson:

*Several years ago when my daughter was pregnant, she was working on a circle island tour bus that would go down at 4:00 in the morning and pick up the tourists and take them down to the airport. This particular morning at about 4:00 when she woke up, I kissed her good-bye and went back to sleep. While I was asleep I saw myself in her van, sitting on the right side of the bus, and I could hear the people talking, about seven of them in the bus, and I noticed she was falling asleep. So, I said to her in the dream, "Wake up, Hana. You are falling asleep, you are losing control of your van." Well, she just fell and slumped over the wheel. So I reached over, in the dream once more, and I pressed the brake down hard. You would expect the car to stop, but it did not. It went around a concrete embankment instead and it climbed around, and then I woke up. I*

*went to work that day and at night I came home. She was*
*cooking dinner for her husband. . . . I said, "Did you fall*
*asleep at the wheel of your van this morning? She said, "Yes,*
*I did. I fell asleep." . . . So I asked "When you woke up, where*
*were you?" She said, "I was coming up a concrete ramp at the*
*airport." . . . I said, "Where did you fall asleep? She said,*
*"Well, the last I remember is the Bishop Museum." . . . The*
*Bishop Museum is quite a distance from the airport, and there*
*is a critical junction where you have to select the right ramp*
*to get on the freeway to go down. You have to reject the lowest*
*one and the highest one and take the middle one.From the*
*Bishop Museum to the airport she had . . . been asleep. . . . This*
*is another dimension to reality. . . . (Johnson, quoted in Friesen*
*1991, 11)*

Johnson's experience reminds that there is really no meaningful
category in Western experience to codify all the subliminal or
supraliminal "forms" present in the Native world.

If Johnson's world may be called "white magic," because it is
life-enhancing, there is also the world of "black magic," whose effects are life-threatening. In William Ferea's report on Melanesian
sorcery, for example, "contagious magic" is described in which
negative spells or conditions may be cast. By condemning a piece
of clothing, or a lock of hair, or even the footprint of one's victim,
one may engender physical harm, as if by contagious contami-
nation. Even pointing a bone or staring intently at a "victim"
may have severe physical and psychological effects. Once again,
forms such as the rituals of contagious magic, including voodoo,
make little sense without understanding the larger context. In
this case the spiritual context could involve either the destructive
use of (positive) spirits or the use of destructive spirits.

## SACRED PLACE

Communication forms make little sense without reference to where they are practiced. Some rituals were never performed outside a specific locale; others could be used only in specific *types* of environments. Here is a description of such specific communication sites in the fieldwork of Diane Bell among central Australian Aboriginals:

> *Through ... overlapping and interlocking modes of expression about how one is "of the land," Central Australian women and men locate themselves within the ancestral design. (Bell 1991, 264–266)*
>
> *When women wish to engage in* yawulyu, *or serious discussion concerning* yawulyu *places, women retire to their ceremonial ground. Situated ... conceptually "in the bush," and thus beyond the settlement, are the ritual shore-house, bough-shelter and "ring place" ceremonial ground. This area is inaccessible by road, and not visible from the residential camps. Men travel circuitous routes to avoid even sighting the general area, and women, if disturbed by children during ritual activity at the "ring place," will carry through disciplinary threats which at other times, because of the high levels of personal autonomy enjoyed by children, are not enforced. (Bell 1991, 9–10)*

Bell describes several qualities of the women's sacred setting —seclusion, protection, distance, exclusiveness (to women), privacy, and specific purpose. In the ceremonial ground, private thoughts and special rites may be expressed without male eavesdropping or interference. An atmosphere of female interchange through ritual song and conversation is sustained.

Groups of men, too, had sacred sites, as did healers, chiefs, tribes, and even intertribal councils. Some ceremonies, songs, and stories could only be expressed "on location," by virtue of their sacredness, association with the place, exclusivity (by gender, age, or profession), or simply due to tradition. In the Shuswap and Carrier sweat lodges, for example, different ceremonies were sung and spoken, just as unique liturgies were used in Episcopal and Roman Catholic masses.

I can remember being invited to hear and sing songs in Shuswap men's sweat lodges. Reportedly, the songs were not sung elsewhere or in mixed company. On the one hand, the sweat lodge provided a more *sacred* atmosphere for the Shuswap men to congregate, like the cloistered chapel of monasteries. On the other hand, the lodge provided a private place for men to socialize in a less inhibited, robust manner, not unlike a college fraternity or football locker room. Some Shuswap stated that the sweat lodge tradition provided an isolated place for sacred male communion.

Summarily, although each form listed below will be isolated for better understanding, it would have been used in a specific context which imbued it with greater meaning. Each form would have drawn life from the philosophy and purpose imbued within it, through the sacred site where it was perpetually reborn from the enhanced perception of the observer, and through the spirit(s), both human and Superhuman, within and surrounding it.

## Types of Communication

*Many moons ago the Indians had a method of communication known as Indian telegraphy. One hour after Custer and his army were wiped out, an Indian in the U.S. Camp gave the message to the camp: "Yellow Hair and all army wiped out."*

*It took the runner three days to bring the official news—the same message. No one knew just how that message was first sent. All over New England there were bounding rocks. With these, the Indians sent messages, by a code, for miles. These were huge rocks, hollowed out underneath so they would send a sound when flat stones were moved on them. (Red Wing St. Cur 1976, 354)*

Such telegraphic stones, now sometimes called "cup and saucer" rocks, are reminiscent of a large number of forgotten, seemingly "magical" types of communication. While prehistoric rock carvings, from Scandinavia to the Alps, have been identified and photographed for textbooks, "talking stones" have disappeared into rock formations as the familiar furniture of nature. While Egyptian hieroglyphics and hieratic Mesopotamian cuneiform are available in museums, Native lance communication—in which the specific vertical, diagonal, and horizontal movements of a warrior's lance communicated messages—is seldom on display. Below are some of the known species of Native communication.

### BLAZING ARROWS

In North America, arrow shafts, or a flammable material wrapped near the arrowhead, were ignited by a Native archer. By night or at dusk the height and arc of the flaming arrow could signal a variety of messages, including location, an event, "danger," or a ceremonial meaning (Fronval and Dubois 1978, 72).

### BODY TATTOO

While some type of tattooing was found on most continents, the elaborate full body tattoos of groups such as the Marquesas

Islanders gave evidence of tattoo complexity and beauty. Depending on tribe and location, tattooing could communicate any or all of the following meanings: genealogy, social status, protection against evil spirits, archetypal symbolism, and personal kinship, or tribal history (Polynesian Cultural Center Exhibit, Oahu, 1991).

## FACIAL AND BODY PAINTINGS

Often misnamed "war paint," facial and body makeup had many purposes, depending on the location, tribe, and type of ceremony. Facial paintings often represented or imitated specific animal features, such as the wearer's guardian spirit (i.e., the Coyote, Bear, Hawk). Often markings suggested parts of the environment, such as the clouds or sunset, or symbolized deities. The images of two leaders or brothers might be coordinated or complementary. Battles were only one occasion for painted faces, hands, chests, legs, or genitals. Rites of passage, healings, and other ceremonies featured unique makeup. Sometimes the markings even signified an attitude, such as "vindictiveness is over" or "beware" or "peace." "Paint," like "war," was part of the misnomer, since dyes, berry stains, clay amalgams, and other temporary colorings, rather than permanent "paints," were primarily used (Boaz 1969).

## TRAIL SIGNS

In all continents nature markings were used by trackers, scouts, warriors, shamans, hunters, and others. Some were for the purpose of internal communication; if, for example, a scout scraped the bark of every tenth tree, he could easily retrace his steps. Other markings were for the purpose of external communication; for example, a snake drawn on a stone might indicate that

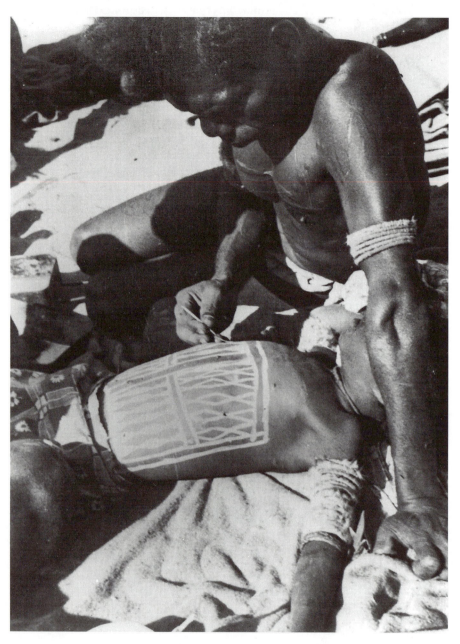

*Body painting as part of an initiation ceremony. From* Aborigines in the Northern Territory *(Milton, Queensland, Australia: Jacaranda Press), 1974.*

quicksand lies beyond. Although most scout markings—broken oak twigs, small rock piles, a leaf speared with a branch tip—were simple, they constituted an entire language. Many trail signs eluded the untrained eye and thus formed a secret Native code (Fronval and Dubois 1978, 72).

## FEATHER LANGUAGE

Feather adornments are found in almost every location inhabited by fowl. Displayed almost everywhere—on the head, buckskins, drums, pipes, weapons, and ceremonial costumes—they had individual and collective meaning. Some were a means of parading achievements, such as the first or second to kill an enemy or the most courageous during a vision quest. Others might signify rank, role, family, or seniority within the group. For many North American tribes the eagle feather symbolized the Great Spirit (or Wonkantonka) and carried the deepest significance. Because of the elaborate web of meaning constructed by careful selection and arrangement, it was a major insult for a white person to steal, destroy, or ignore a feathered headdress. In some ceremonies feathers were used as detached symbols or props, sometimes waved or upheld to invoke spirits, invite prosperity, or effect healing (Fronval and Dubois 1978, 73).

## LIVING IDOLS AND ICONS

Throughout the world statues with supernatural faces, hybrid bodies (half man half animal), and symbolic markings have survived. From wood, stone, clay, and numerous other materials Aboriginal Peoples carved and molded likenesses of gods. In most cases, such idols and icons were thought to be alive or possessed of the spirit of the god portrayed. In the Marquesas, "Tiki" meant *a* god, while "Kon-Tiki" meant a *great* god. In a sacred setting, large wooden "Tiki" or "Kon-Tiki" likenesses might protect or guard the setting. It is difficult to separate such sculptures from "crafts" such as masks, pottery, and shields, which also embodied or accommodated specific spirits (Polynesian Cultural Center Exhibit, Oahu, 1991).

## WALKING AND TALKING STICKS

The elaborate carvings or fine wood found on a stick used for *walking* (and display) indicated that it gave more than physical support. Such a stick might be used in ritually approaching plants, in honoring the spirits carved on the stick, and in warding off intruding phantoms. A *talking* stick, by contrast, was held in the hand when it was one's turn to speak at a council or event. This stick was passed from person to person, usually from man to man, when opinions were considered about tribal affairs (interview, Grim 1/18/91, Archie 5/10/92).

## TALKING DRUMS

While most Native people developed some type of percussion instruments, the "talking drums" of Africa were especially effective. Such drums, located in each tribe or village, seemed magical since drummers learned to hear and relay distant drumming *instantly:* in concert, the drums could send any message many miles almost simultaneously across many stations. So elaborate was the drum coding that any message could be transferred, as with Morse code, hence the name "talking drums." Often the communication was "binary"; it played on the interaction of two drums in counterpoint, alternating between high note and low note. Occasionally, other instruments, such as a two-tone horn or

*The Deer Dance has been danced for centuries by the Pueblo Indians in New Mexico. This Deer Dance is at San Ildefonso Pueblo, 1991. Photograph © by Marcia Keegan.*

whistle, were substituted. Talking drums were no more "primitive" than telegrams or telephones and reached a far wider audience (Carrington 1949, 8–10).

## POETRY

Although it is often difficult to separate Native poetry from song, chant, and storytelling, there are distinctive poetic genres of spoken rhythmic beauty. In Tonga, for example, nature poetry summons the poet to be *concrete* by verbally conjuring images of real places with which she is familiar. Such poems evoke the beauty of and oneness with nature. In some traditions there is no barrier between poetry and song such that the shaman may speak and sing lines alternatively or speak, then chant. Many myths are presented in language ripe with symbol, imagery, oral repetitions, silences, infrequent alliterations, metered rhythm, and occasional rhyme. In storytelling there is no fence between poetry and prose (interview, Helu 1/18/91).

## BLANKET LANGUAGES

A blanket was never worn haphazardly. It might convey the age, stage, status, or history of its owner. And its design might say much more than was at first apparent, for most blankets had symbols, stories, attitudes, or owner identification markings embedded within their colors and shapes (Fronval and Dubois 1978, 73).

## HORSE AND PONY COMMUNICATION

In many locations horses and ponies were painted or decorated, often in colors and manner that matched their riders. From a distance, the painted markings or feathers on an approaching horse

All's well

Good hunting!

Help! Danger!

Attack

*Examples of Native American smoke signals. Drawings © by Michael Ottersen.*

might convey who his former rider was and in which battle he was killed. Animals also communicated by means of their movements. For example, a horse on a clifftop might move two paces to his left, or rise up on his hind legs twice, meaning that a rider is nearby, that buffalo are over the hill, or that a rival band is approaching. Such a signal, whether given by a mounted or a lone horse, would be invisible, like a well-marked deck of cards, to oncoming cavalry or rival tribes (Archives, Rock Point School 1990).

## SMOKE SIGNALS

Although frequently trivialized in Westerns, smoke signals were very effective. By alternatively covering a pyramid of branches with a blanket and then removing the blanket, within a precise rhythm, signalers could direct spirals of smoke from high altitudes. By using different intervals between signals and different size spirals, a sort of smoke shorthand was developed. One cloud might mean "be careful"; two, "all is well"; three, "help." Since fires could be built at high altitudes, two tribes on either side of a mountain could use signals at a shared station near the mountain peak to communicate about special ceremonies, advancing troops, or "wedding" invitations. (Fronval and Dubois 1978, 72).

## NAMES

Relatively few tribes employed Western-style "family" names according to parentage ("the son of Uliki," "the daughter of Fulu") or trade ("deer stalker," "the one who makes bracelets with hands"). Usually naming carried deeper spiritual and personal significance by identifying the essential character trait or spirit of the one named—"courageous singer of tales," "heroic oak," "comforter of those who mourn"—or the essential trait of one's guardian animal or essence—"fearless bear," "warming sun," "gentle elk." In many groups final names were not given until adolescence or adulthood, such that the name may be earned and awarded at a rite of passage. In Hawaii, the names of high chiefs were kapu (sacred) and thus forbidden to be used by others, or in some cases, even forbidden to be spoken. Rules and traditions about names varied widely, but the sense that a name was attached to core identity, not an abstract label, was universal (Tatar 1982, 17).

## DANCE

In *Tristes Tropiques,* Claude Lévi-Strauss noted many parallels between Brazilian Native ceremonies and those in North America (Lévi-Strauss 1981, 220–228). While unique within most tribes, dancing featured structures and essences (mourning, celebration, narrative, greeting, worship) practiced worldwide. The wide variety of attitudes employed in dance may be suggested through this short list of Polynesian traditional dances:

| DANCE | PEOPLE | PURPOSE/ATTITUDE |
| --- | --- | --- |
| Patua | Maori | women show dexterity; men convey disdain |
| Ku'uhoa | Hawaiian | romantic emotions for companion |
| Bibi na senico | Fiji | male call to battle and boldness |
| Ma'ulu'ulu | Tongan | deep appreciation for island heritage |
| Oite amui a | Tahitian | joyful women welcome loved ones from battle |
| Mother's Dance | Samoan | older women pass skills to younger ones |

In Polynesia and Micronesia the full range of human emotion is displayed through literally hundreds of Native dances. In many, men compete with dangerous props such as flaming sticks or knives, while women are more likely to perform dances about love, beauty, domestic responsibilities, and nature (Polynesian Cultural Center Exhibit, Oahu 1991, 4–5).

*Papua, New Guinea. Mekeo dancers with drums. Negative #338005. Courtesy Department of Library Services, American Museum of Natural History.*

In the Americas and Africa, virtually every natural phenomenon has its dance. Each season, event, individual, act of nature, crop, disease, plant, animal, insect, stage of life, spirit, attitude, place, and celestial body is honored by at least a few, and in some cases hundreds, of tribes. Throughout the world dance costumes and masks draw on decorative flowers, herbs, grasses, woods, and other materials to exude color, atmosphere, and attitudes. Instrumentation ranging from a solo conch shell or hollowed whistle to a group of fifty hourglass drummers might accompany or participate in the dancing (interview, Rapu 1/11/91).

## SONG

As with dance, song is ubiquitous in Aboriginal societies. Grim (interview 1/18/91) has noted tribes in which "everything has a song—animals, plants, and beyond." Momaday and Curtis make song central to the Indigenous experience: "to the Indian, song is the breath of the spirit that consecrates the acts of life" (Curtis 1987). The uses of song are diverse as when Sullivan (1989) notes their healing nature on the one hand—"one can hardly overstate the power of song, especially rhythmic ceremonial chant, in South American medicine" (405)—and their creative power on the other—"for the Karina of Venezuela, every sound creates a species [which] is why each species makes its own sound" (406). Song is equally commonplace in both the lore of creation, as when gods sang the world into existence, and in the ways in which such lore is regenerated. Noted forms of Native singing include unison, gender separate, choral chant, solo chant, repetitive raga, antiphonal male/female, ceremonial falsetto, adult choral, a capella, accompanied, and human/animal counterpoint (see Curtis, Grim, Momaday, Sullivan, Red Wing St. Cur).

## TOTEM POLES

A totem was an animal (likeness) considered related to a family or group by blood. Like a patron saint, a totem possessed the powers to uniquely assist or safeguard its ward. A Native might meet his unique totem during a vision quest or another solitary encounter with nature. Or the totem might be passed from generation to generation. Likenesses of totems could be found in sculpture, painting, carving, and the designs of tepees, lodges, boats, and clothing. When white settlers of the Pacific Northwest discovered tall wooden poles with several totems carved from top to bottom, "totem poles" became the common name for the guardposts. The term "low man on the totem pole" meaning "at the bottom of the pecking order" was a white misnomer, since the chief at the bottom of the pole was usually protected by the guards or scout totems at the top. Totem poles served various functions—mortuary (commemorating deaths), genealogical (family history), confrontational (protecting against adversaries or apparitions), and landmark (to mark an occasion such as a potlatch). Not unlike a family crest or coat of arms, the family's most important heraldry was protected and thus appeared at the bottom (Smyly and Smyly 1973).

## SIGN LANGUAGE

Hand language was featured in the Hawaiian hula dance, in African greetings, in South American hunting signals, and in North American intertribal communication and may have been ubiquitous. In some cases, the hands were used to touch others, as when the New Guinea Dani men reach out to touch the testicles of another man as a greeting. But in most cases, the signs involved touching self or extending the hands outward while

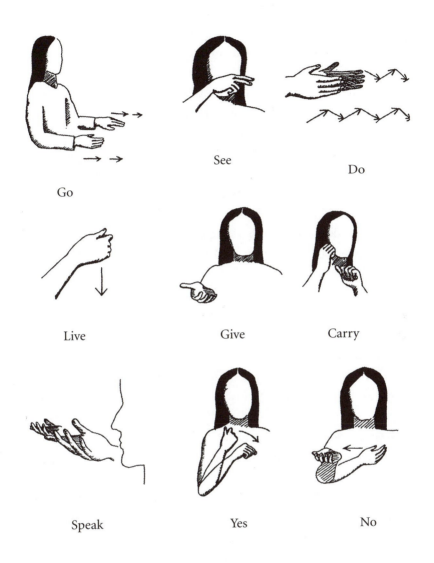

Examples of Native American sign language. Drawings © by Michael Ottersen.

employing a series of finger and thumb gestures. Many tribes
had "internal" (i.e., exclusive to the tribe) gestures, such as hunters
might silently use when stalking animals to avoid making sounds.
A more frequent sign language, however, was used as a common
code between tribes, so they could communicate despite having
different spoken languages. When warriors, hunters, or scouts
from different tribes met in the woods, they could settle disputes,
barter, exchange news, or arrange to divide venison through a
series of hand gestures. Needless to say, Native populations also
contained deaf and nonspeaking people who used hand signals,
possibly before Westerners "invented" the language of the deaf
(see Fronval, Teit).

## A UNIVERSE OF FORMS

Limitations of space make it impossible to discuss the multitude
of other Native communication forms. Consider, for example, the
plethora of household traditions such as a Maori father placing
water on the brow of his children to say "be careful today" to each
one as she awakens (interview, Hopa 1/19/91). Also consider the
many mysterious forms such as the Cogi's mapped lines carved in
stone, which represent lines of thought, rather than paths or
roads. Consider, too, the twenty-four-hour debates that were a test
of endurance. Another form, weeping, is ritualized in some communities to commemorate the weeping of the gods when they left
the earth (interview, Sullivan 1/19/91).

Laughter is intrinsic to most societies, frequently subtle and
often an "inside joke" requiring explanation (Maestas 307). The
communication forms surrounding sorcery and evil spirit magic
are numerous, as are the more positive forms of healing, such as
blowing on the body, sucking evil spirits out of the sick, incanta-
tions, and dropping amulets on diseased areas. Finally, among

the hundreds of other forms are storytelling, white magic, basket weaving, hissing, spear waving, telepathic emotion transfer, sandstone drawing, bloodletting, sun worship, medicine wheels, medicine shields, throat clicking, body scarring, genital sculpture, lip stretching, nose piercing, bird calling, owl dialogue, ritual copulation, torch twirling, female fertility rites, cave backdrop painting, and animal mimicry. Several of these will be discussed below.

## TECHNIQUE AND FUNCTION

The term "primitive" connotes not only "unsophisticated" and "earliest" but also "rough," "crude," and "undeveloped." Thus "primitive" communication was often portrayed by the early explorers as "coarse" and "unpolished." In the Western mythology about Native communication, all Natives seemed to resemble the cave man, and to epitomize the amateur's approach to expression.

But this characterization could not be further from the truth. In India, young boys learning sacred ceremonies had to precisely shape their mouths for several hours every day while elders disciplined them after each incorrect sound. A young Navajo could not become a healer (medicine man) unless he was willing to learn each ceremony with fine precision. Nor could he take shortcuts when singing specific chants at the side of the afflicted, sometimes for several consecutive days and nights. For central Plains tribes the fate of one's family might depend on the construction of the tepee, canoe, or bow, so artistic *perfection* was encouraged.

Thus, contrary to stereotype, "primitive" communication was unusually precise, unwavering, highly stylized, and well disciplined. In observing movement in the performing arts of the Pacific islands, Adrienne Kaeppler (1986) looked beyond first impressions. At first glance, Pacific dances seemed to involve only "a fluid movement of the arms and legs." On closer inspection Kaeppler spotted a rotation of the lower arm, a flexion and extension of the wrist, exact curling of the fingers, matched bending elbows, and simultaneous flexion of the knuckles (590). The degree of difficulty and refinement of some dances might compare with Olympic synchronized figure skating, multiplied by thirty people.

Simpler dances, such as belligerent war prances (in which men leap forward suggesting ferocity and macho strength) might require fewer body movements but necessitate internal group choreography, endurance, and athletic prowess. If not precisely rendered, the more dangerous dances, those involving the juggling or throwing of flaming weapons, wrapping of dancers with poisonous snakes, hanging by tethered skin, leaping across elevated ledges, or jumping on hot coals, could end in tragedy.

Nor was the composition of Indigenous music mere guesswork. Native Hawaiian music required the matching of sweetened harmonies with slurred, soothing melodies, which outered the natural atmosphere of tropical denizens. Every ingredient within the gentle expression emphasized fluidity: hand gestures were smooth, rather than angular; composition involved no minor, diminished, or atonal constructions, only major and major-seventh chords; voices were tender, sometimes soprano falsetto; instruments, such as the Hawaiian guitar and (imported) ukulele, emphasized soft, bending notes; in chants, the many open vowels at the ends of words let the tones float away and ascend, unlike consonants, which would close off the breath and fragment the sound stream. Indeed, all the musical elements created a unified style that captured the pacific flowing expression.

Native Canadian Bill Wilson implies that even conversation served a variety of functions: "Our oral tradition is not only to pass on history. It's to get to know people. It just makes so much sense we can sit down with an elder and he or she is going to tell you their life story, their history" (Bill Wilson, First Nations Congress, 1985). History was transferred, people became friends, traditions were preserved, and a common identity was sensed simply through dialogue. Chant was a type of therapy during times of crisis but more like consecration at major occasions such as births, puberty rites, and home blessings (Bierhost 1983, 3). At a death ceremony, chant seemed more cathartic, or, in some tribes, celebratory.

Prayer, too, as in virtually all societies, might have a variety of functions—acknowledgment of divinity, relieving anxiety, blessing a particular person or place, gaining control over others, attempting to be successful (at the harvest, at the hunt, on a quest, etc.), summoning forth a specific spirit, unifying the tribe, changing the atmosphere, casting out evil spirits, or, when misused, showing off.

But this is to speak only of *oral* prayer. As Natalie Curtis points out, *visual* prayer "is conveyed in designs of woven fabrics, in beadwork, pottery, and decorations of all kinds, in dance, in ceremony, and in song" (1989–1987). Hence the functions of prayer expand through numerous pictorial and animated forms.

When the function of a form was highly specialized, an exacting procedure was necessary. For example, when creating a sand painting, the Navajo healer had to draw the painting during the ceremony, precisely discern and render the appropriate drawing, conceal the image from the sick person until its completion, and then destroy the picture almost immediately.

Similarly, a shaman of the Pacific Northwest coast had to utilize specific tools and techniques when treating the wounded. In many tribes, he had to dress like the spirit that would possess him, construct and use rattles and masks appropriate to the ceremony, open himself to the supernatural spirit that wished to possess him, become sufficiently "transparent" to be a pure medium for the spirit, then utilize rattler, mask, and specific words to ensure the cure.

Many functions of Native ceremony are relatively obscure, such as the Buluwandi, a central Australian ceremony for the resolution of conflict (Berndt 216), or lesser known forms of the hula, which told the history and literature of their people (Kuualoha 2/1/91). Words had a variety of obscure functions, such as voicing absolute creative commands (charged with unwavering power), regenerating the impotent, invoking magic spells, and exorcising demons. Some American Natives used "soft words," words spoken quietly or whispered to superhuman spirits, lest they be overheard. Often the meaning of "soft words" was somewhat hidden, so that a person and a spirit could maintain private conversation (Bierhorst 1983, 4).

## INFLUENCE OF NATIVE FORMS

While the primary function of Aboriginal communication might be called intercourse with the sacred, numerous forms seemed more secular, such as telling an animal anecdote (a popular genre within Native jokes) or harassing an enemy band with battle shrieks. Many forms, both secular and sacred, have infused "Western civilization" with life. The U.S. city council, security council, and other councils, for example, were anteceded not only by European councils but by Native tribal and intertribal councils. A "moment of silence" to remember the dead has several Native precedents. Modern dances have incorporated or reproduced innumerable indigenous African, South American, and Native American rhythms, animal mimicry, and movements. Indigenous art, whether incorporated by the primitivists of Europe or copied by Western painters and collectors today, is found far beyond the boundaries of reservations. Authentic Native costuming and especially jewelry infuses the fashion trends of Europe, Asia, and the Americas.

It is somewhat ironic that the misrepresentative symbol of Native communication—a chief raising his open hand and saying "How"—was in response to the white man's influence on the Native. The Indigenous vocabulary did not include "How." But, since the settler and the soldier asked the Native so many questions—"How are you doing?" "How is your family?" "How are your crops?" "How is your health?"—the Native sought to nullify this lengthy examination with one simple "How?" This shorthand for "How are your affairs?" posed to the white intruder was a courteous acknowledgment of the "white man's greeting," neatly compressed into the more laconic Native style.

Whatever the specific influence of the two cultures, oral and literate, upon each other, the more general, overarching influence of Native communication on modern society has been overlooked. This larger contribution is best expressed in the words of Princess Red Wing St. Cur:

> *The Indians never received credit for all their contributions to civilization. . . . On the aesthetic side stand beauty in sculpture and architecture, beauty in traditional literature of myths, song and rituals, poems, beauty in dance and spectacular ceremonies, and beauty above all in the ethical and philosophical attitude of man towards man and toward nature.*
>
> *Although it is easy to show the useful gifts of the Indian, since more than half of the present agricultural wealth of the U.S. comes from the plants which he tamed, it is not easy to estimate the influence of his aesthetic on the present culture of his conquerors, but the coming effect will surely be very great. (Red Wing St. Cur 1976, 354)*

*Australian Aboriginal didgeridoo players. From* Aborigines in the Northern Territory. *(Milton, Queensland: Jacaranda Press), 1974.*

# CHAPTER FOUR

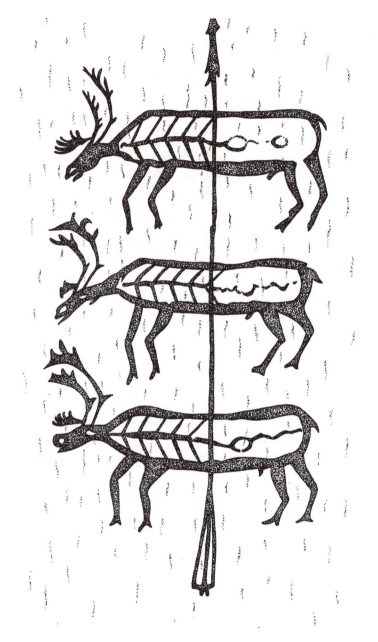

*Caribou painted on an Inuit wooden bowl are ritually "killed" by an arrow. This skeletal depiction shows the animal's soul, which resides in the bladder and bones. Bones are treated with respect, so the animal can return to feed people. Drawing © by Sabra Moore.*

# Communication
# Ethics

Native Peoples had innumerable unique laws, rules, customs, and ethical practices that distinguished their communication from that of the European explorers. For example, when eating together, members of most literate societies choose to sit facing each other, often at a table; the Algonquin people, however, did *not* face each other when eating as it was considered rude and coarse to do so (Wescott 9/21/90). It was unthinkable for a Shuswap band member to speak disrespectfully to a tribal elder— quite the opposite of the manner in which Sam Donaldson or Barbara Walters might approach a U.S. political leader. Whereas the ethical mandate of the American press includes serving as watchdog for the American people, which might justify skeptical cross-examination of even the U.S. president, the Shuswap communication ethic mandated that one spoke to everyone, especially elders, with great respect.

In this chapter, I will explore Indigenous ethics, rules, laws, and customs as they relate to communication. The primary definitions for these terms are:

- *ethics:* standards of moral conduct and judgment; way of life
- *custom:* traditional convention enforced by social
    (dis)approval

- *law:* formal rule usually *physically enforced* by community authority
- *rule:* established principal that determines behavior; fixed guide for conduct

Since this book is not an elaborate treatise on the semantic differences among these terms, I wish to simplify their relationship. Since laws, rules, and ethics *may* fall within the rubric "cultural customs," the term "customs" will be perceived as redundant and seldom helpful for our purposes. Communication *rules* will pertain to *all* guidelines for communication behavior. Communication *ethics* refers to that subset of rules that is moral in nature, while communication law refers to that subset of rules that is physically enforced by community authority. Communication law and communication ethics are overlapping subsets of the large universe of communication rules.

For example, if Ubangi children are taught never to shout without explanation, they are being taught a communication rule. If they are taught never shout into a person's ear or it will hurt them, they are being taught a communication ethic of compassion and respect. Finally, if they are taught never to shout into a person's ear lest they will be stoned by the chief and elders, they are being taught a law. Naturally, it is possible that a rule may be both ethical and legal, such as "Never shout into a person's ear, lest he be hurt and you be stoned."

Before we proceed to consideration of rules, law, and ethics, it is worthwhile to reiterate that these are not Native categories and thus are meaningless in many Indigenous cultures. For some tribes, all communication seems natural, not socially imposed, so whatever socialized behavior members exhibit is at once automatically ethical, legal, and customary. There are no alternative behaviors. Notions of morality and ethics are relative; if in one society it is unethical to eat human flesh, in a society of cannibals it might be unethical *not* to taste from the Native menu. Finally, societies extend from the authoritarian extreme—in which virtually all rules are enforced by ethics *and* law—to the almost anarchic—in which the only rule is to maintain an ethic against law.

Having considered all these caveats and remembering that every rule has an exception, let us consider the communication rules, laws, and ethics of Native people. Throughout this consideration it is wise to remember that, depending on the culture, at least two of these terms may slightly or entirely overlap. It is equally wise to note that, within the inherently spiritual world of Indigenous People, at one level all rules pertain to a larger ethic and Divine Law.

## Rules of Communication

In tribal societies, rules of communication may be exacting and particular. For example, among the Wampar people of Melanesia, the "thou shalt nots" include (1) never turn your back on your cousins or your in-laws; (2) never swear at your wife in front of her parents; (3) never sing a song composed by someone outside your clan, unless or until the clan members join in first; (4) (for young boys and women) never discuss an initiation ceremony in which you have participated (interview, Ferea 1/18/91). If you violate the first rule (back-turning), the only penalty is an apology. However, if you break the second rule, a more serious penalty— killing a pig to ease embarrassment—is expected.

While few such rules are absolutely enforced by a central legal authority, each could be associated with a Western ethical doctrine: rule 1 reminds of notions of secrecy and respect; rule 2 pertains to obscenity, defamation, and abuse; rule 3 points toward notions of censorship, ownership, and copyright; rule 4 raises questions of privacy, censorship (again), and even the freedom of information policy.

Rules often pertain to the job description of roles or art forms. For example, a shaman may never show his face during the ceremonies of one tribe; in another tribe, he may only use his animal voice. And "in southern Nigeria, Adj carvers work in isolation while observing certain prohibitions, and Isoko dancers always wear protective medicines while performing" (Peek 1981, 20).

In viewing the documentary films of Robert Gardner, who has filmed dozens of groups of Indigenous Peoples worldwide, one is left with the hypothesis that some general communication rules are universal: each group seems to have taboo topics, attitudes toward protecting reputation, enforced or expected silences, gender rules, children's norms, and notions of bad taste or obscenity. According to Gardner, "Obscenity seems variable in its definition but generic in its existence" (interview 9/20/90). This suggests that there may be "universals" within Indigenous communication just as Freud suggested universal taboos (for example, against incest and parricide) within all societies.

One suggested universal is that "there are some different communication rules for women and men." Gender-based rules are ubiquitous. There are even languages spoken only by women or men. Diane Bell reveals how certain communications were available to her from Aboriginal women which would not have been available to either Aboriginal or visiting men:

> *Because of the sex-segregated nature of Aboriginal society, it is extremely inappropriate . . . to work equally with men and women. Usually one is identified with members of one's own sex and is able to move freely within that sphere. Fortunately for my study, women considered my position agreeable for one who sought ritual instruction. . . . I was economically*

*and emotionally independent of men and therefore poten-*
*tially safe with women's secrets. Further, the social status I*
*enjoyed by virtue of my two outgoing and energetic children*
*allowed me access to the world of adult women. Ritual knowl-*
*edge resides with the older women who . . . devote their time*
*and energies to upholding and transmitting their spiritual*
*heritage to successive generations. (1991, 7)*

Women of specific ages and status could communicate about subjects that others could not. Many cultures restrict the secretive transmitting of spiritual heritage to small groups of men, while others have two secret societies, male *and* female.

Rules often safeguard generic communication events. For example, in conflict resolution, each tribe has a distinctive approach for the event Westerners might call a verbal dispute. Among the Maori people, who may discuss issues for days until consensus is reached, it is implicit that the door must always be left open for disputants to leave a conflict with dignity. (interview, Hopa 1/14/91) A "joking debate" is employed among Fijians (Arno 1993) and "emotion talk" is used on the Solomon Islands (Watson-Gegeo and White 1990). Many cultures seem to provide a ritualistic mode of "disentangling," which avoids the need to resort to violence.

## COMMUNICATION RULES AS SOCIAL CEMENT

Andrew Arno (1993) suggests that each band of Fiji Natives creates and maintains communities by highly regulated communication etiquette. Overlapping systems of communication rules, centered respectively on family, island, community, and region, regulate the Fijian social world. In such societies, communication rules become a primary means of control, not a secondary mode of ancillary behavior. Such rules may pertain (by Western definition) to ethical topics such as defamation of character, obscenity, censorship, and sexual discrimination. There is great clarity and specificity in defining what may be said about others, who are housed within tightly circumscribed roles. For example, in some tribes, joking about and with some cousins is welcome, but joking among and about others would be an insult.

Notions of indecent language are determined by role. For example, in some groups, some cousins may discuss sexual matters, but it is obscene for brothers and sisters to do so.

To talk with in-laws, especially on certain topics, may be prohibited. Often talking occurs through intermediates. In some tribes, a husband may talk to his mother-in-law only if holding a blanket between them so as to nullify eye contact, or through an intermediary.

Men *and* women often have a separate circuit of talk. Segregation by gender may also be by generation and gender. Often one sex is allowed to discuss subjects forbidden for the other sex.

James Ritchie, an expert on the Maoris of New Zealand, reports that much Maori behavior could also fit within the categories of Western "ethics" of communication. In Maori society to turn one's back and show one's rear is considered rude. Demeaning others is unacceptable (Maoris say "I can ward off the physical sphere, but I cannot deflect the word"); indeed, to insult another brings consequences on one's self (interview, Ritchie 1/12/91).

## HIGHER-ORDER RULES

Some rules relate to a subtle spiritual understanding seemingly less common in Western society. For example, among the Maori, it is impolite to ask direct questions, not because of arbitrary custom but because "the mana flows from the greater [person] to the lesser. To question is to usurp the mana and take charge of the flow" (interview, Ritchie 1/11/91). All communication takes place in the energy field of mana. Thus rules of communication derive from a respect for the sacred, and for those carrying the greatest mana.

In Polynesia there are "respect languages" or "high languages" that are spoken for specific occasions or by people of high status. Just as there are two types of language, there are two types of word—ordinary word and sacred word, which is ancestral. Thus to address ancestral matters is to ascend into the arena of tabu (or, in some tribes, kapu), or, in other words, to enter the "guarded" or "contained" areas of high discussion.

Such rules of using higher or inner languages were not unusual to Native Americans, who frequently deflected the questions of settlers as if to say "that is a sacred area I cannot discuss with you." And some matters could be discussed in Polynesia only *after* specific shared experiences. Then and only then was a person considered trustworthy. For example, if a white scout helped build several sweat lodges, only *after* their completion might he find out what is said inside the lodge.

Higher-order rules are also associated with the Aboriginals. To evoke the spirit of an ancestor, for example, an Aboriginal would first need to own "the rights" to that ancestor via specific kinship. Second, prior to the ceremony, specific people would need to be summoned to attend. Third, the correct ceremony would be required. Finally, the person summoning an ancestor would need to be in residence at the correct location. Ancestors will not return unless the rules are properly followed (interview, Bell 1/11/91).

In such societies, speech has its own rules. When a Native dies in Central Australia often sign language will be respectfully substituted for speech, which is often suspended "in dangerous times." Indeed some mourners would be lost without sign language, since the period of silence may last up to two years. All words are sacred in many tribes and closely associated with the spirit of what they describe. Indeed, in Central Australia, Aboriginals "retire" not only the names of the dead but also words and phrases that sound similar or might evoke the dead spirit.

Higher rules of communication have practical purposes. For example, a simple forgetting to pronounce a "benediction" at the close of a worship ritual could be devastating. By virtue of the innocent oversight, both the absent-minded individual and the entire community would remain unprotected until the next benediction. Failure to remember which words are tabu is like ignoring the Danger sign at the gate of a nuclear reactor. A communication mixup could be slanderous, scandalous, or even lethal.

## CHILDREN'S RULES AND LEARNING

Children's education both utilized and taught communication rules. Although a Shuswap magical story about Coyote and Bear might seem entertaining, it would also imply a moral that reinforced the Shuswap way of life. Coyote might be punished if he did not fully respect the Old One (God the Creator) in the story, so the storyteller might reinforce the message "Respect the Elders: do not walk in front of them or talk in their presence. If you do, you'll be ridiculed like Coyote."

While storytelling was a favorite means of teaching rules in many societies, the Native largely taught by example. Most schools were "experiential": one learned to be quiet when stalking a giraffe, not in a schoolroom, but by observing older spearsmen in the hunting parties. Since many extended families lived together in one hut, tepee, wigwam, igloo, or lodge, toddlers could observe virtually all the communication rules of society—how to treat elders, how to treat parents, how to communicate during sex, how to speak to the same and the opposite sex—within one dwelling.

But communication rules were also taught through specific rewards and punishments. Just as the settler's children might have their mouths washed out with a bar of soap for lying, the Native Kawaiian children suffered an even more effective punishment, having hot chile peppers smashed on their tongues. Kawaiian children were also taught never to talk back, not to be tattle-tales, not to interrupt adult conversation, not to mention the genitals (thought to be sacred), and not to talk about events of the future while eating ("one might eat them [future events], too") (interview, R. Johnson 1/14/91).

In some tribes, during pregnancy, the mother was not to speak (negatively) of the child lest it be listening. Similarly, spouses were often taught to avoid critical speech toward their children, even when speaking privately, to ensure good health. Evil words toward others, even when accidentally released, could deform, jinx, damage, or even destroy. So the rules of speaking often had to be *internally* applied: each person was responsible for self-censorship of potentially damaging and defaming statements.

Children were vulnerable to the "wicked words" of mind control, tabu abuse, voodoo misuse, and mana manipulation. In many tribes, just as Western children are now taught to avoid "strangers," Indigenous children were taught to avert their eyes or shut their ears when tribesmen thought to be sorcerers or vindictive rivals walked nearby. In some societies affirmations could be learned, or amulets worn, which protected against evil words and phrases. Since contagious magic would often be exercised against the children of those targeted, young people had to learn at an early age how to avoid "vibrational" harm and seductive charm.

For example, in a tribe in which a sorcerer might harm a child by cursing its footprints, the child would learn to step on leaves or erase the footprints. If a lock of hair could be stolen from a child and then cursed in a voodoo ritual, the child might sleep with parents or have a blessing performed for its hair to protect against hair stealing.

# Laws

Law has been generically defined above as formal rules usually physically enforced by community authority. Since "formal" sometimes implies "written," it is important to remember that oral societies have little concept of "law" as preserved documents. Their physical enforcement, however, could be severe: in *Fragments of Hawaiian History,* John Papa Ji noted that the ancient penalty for a man caught eating coconuts with women (an activity that was kapu) was execution.

In considering anthropological approaches to law, Sally Falk-Moore at Harvard Law School notes that tribal law is usually "social law," that is, it pertains to "the structure of groups," and is an "enforceable system, not just for individuals, but for the group itself." In this sense, "law" is really one social means of control and may be seen in some cases as simply safeguarding the powerful, or protecting the status quo. In authoritarian tribes, law may be seen as those memorized, punitive controls that maintain the hierarchy. Law may often be seen as the most serious subset of rules, carrying the most serious consequences when violations occur.

In more egalitarian, consensus *groups*, law protects group authority against deviance, not just elite authority against rivals. In this sense primal law, no less than civilized law, has a political purpose. Hence communication laws—who may speak to whom and what subjects are taboo—definitely empower some groups (often elders, men, warriors, elite castes, chiefs, adults, or healers), while others (for example, children, women, half-breeds, domestic workers, lower castes, lepers, and widowers) often feel

disempowered and censored. Severe penalties, such as banish-
ment or execution of those who mention tabu (or kapu) subjects,
guarantee strict social control.

To the cosmopolitan, Native laws seem particular and parochial. Clifford Geertz (1983) calls law "local knowledge, local
not just as to place, time, class, and variety of issue, but as to
accent—vernacular characterizations of what happens connect
to vernacular imaginings of what can." Against this perspective
one might juxtapose the "insider" view of law, a more absolutist
view, such as is expressed by the Australian Aborigine Big Bill
Neidjie: "Law never change . . . always stay same. Maybe it hard,
but proper one for all people. Not like white European law . . .
always changing. If you don't like it, you can change. Aboriginal
law never change. Old people tell us, 'You got to keep it.' It always stays" (Neidjie, Davis, and Fox 1986).

From within a society, law does not seem particular and
parochial, but eternal and widespread. Perhaps those who feel
most fatalistic about such eternal law are those trapped in the
Hindu caste system. Castes, which to some degree interpenetrate
tribal societies, treat justice and responsibility as relative to one's
social role. Since social roles are transcendentally defined, it is
impossible for lower caste members to receive equal treatment in
disputes with higher caste members. So as not to romanticize
Indigenous people, it is important to remember that many tribes
had slaves, "apprentices," lesser wives (in polygamous relationships), and captives, who were frequently treated as lower castes
from the Americas to Asia and Africa.

While Western law, with courtrooms and advocates, would
have been foreign to most primal people, systems of dispute
resolution, whether by consensus, chief's ruling, or arbitrated
argument, were not. For a father or leader to help plead one's case,
or for witnesses to be heard, was natural in some societies, and

hearings, such as the two women who pleaded before King Solomon for their baby, seem native to Natives.

Whether described as the "law," or the "way," or the custom, or the "manner" of society, law could take on far grander meaning than dispute resolution. For the Aboriginals, the "law of the dream time" is a cosmic order more akin to the "laws of nature" than to civil law. Diane Bell describes Aboriginal dream time law:

> The Law binds people, flora, fauna and natural phenomena into one enormous inter-functional world. It is the responsibility of the living, who trace direct relationships to these ancestors, to give form and substance to this heritage in their daily routines and their ceremonial practice: to keep the Law, to visit sites, to use the country, and to enjoy its bounty. (1991, 3)

This law is much larger than a canon of regulations and corresponding discipline. Clearly, it is a way a person must be when an ancestral state is invoked, like the ways an actor must be when becoming a character from the fifteenth century. As Bell asserts, "When you put on paint, work with sacred objects, and prepare the Dream ceremony, you become or take on your ancestors" (interview, Bell 1991).

Most studies of Native law are modern. Thus the important research on Zuni law by Watson Smith, John Noon's study of the Iroquois, Richardson's study of the Kiowa, Llewellyn and Hoebel's monographs on the Cheyenne and Comanche, and many others tell us as much about the infusion of Western values as about Native vision. For example, in the cases of the 1940s reported by Smith (1973) about violations of law occurring on Zuni reservations in the U.S. Southwest, Western concepts such as slander are used. However, it is noteworthy that the "communication law" broken, in Zuni terms, predates such Western concepts. Smith refers to law imposed on the Zuni by the U.S. government, but such law was predated by the Zuni's own customs regarding who might speak to whom and in what manner. What is common to both the Western and Zuni systems is a sense of offense surrounding damaged reputation. As Smith states, "Basically, the essence of the offense seems to be an injury to the good name or reputation of an individual through the unsupported accusation of reprehensible conduct" (1973, 56). While Anglo, Hispanic (a culture that colored Zuni traditions), and Zuni procedures differ, all bear a concern for the *honor* of those falsely accused.

Such law may be construed in hybrid terms, that is, as a mixture of the justice systems of Natives and Westerners. Alternatively Law (uppercase L) may mean the rules of the universe, such as a scientist means by the *combined* laws of physics, chemistry, and biology. Or law (lowercase) may refer to specific social rules that are physically enforced by tribal authority when not obeyed. In some situations these types of "law" may overlap. Certainly, they bear a close proximity to ethics, discussed below.

## Ethics, or One Ethic?

One of the overarching meanings of ethics is "a way of life," such as the Buddhist, Marxist, or Judeo-Christian ethic. In this meaning, one school of thought holds that Native People have *an ethic*, that is, an invisible, traditional blueprint for living so inherent it is seldom discussed. Within this ethic there are specific ethics, prescribed standards for moral conduct. Seldom, however, are there tribes that employ the erudite definition of ethics: "a branch of philosophy (definition 3) by which one formally studies the many ways of life (definition 1) and the prescribed standards for moral conduct (definition 2). By and large, Native People have definition 2, but have typically not studied ethics (definition 3).

## A UNIVERSAL CODE OF ETHICS?

While there are tribal differences both in the Native *ethic* and in Native *ethics,* in some ways, Native people have a common moral universe. On that basis, four Native Americans—Judie Bopp, Phil Lane, Lee Brown, and Michael Bopp—assembled their vision of Indigenous ethics. In *The Sacred Tree* they call these "teachings that are universal to all tribes" (1989, 74). These are:

1. The practice of daily sanctification (expressing thankfulness to the Creator(s) (1989, 75).
2. A respect, honor, and esteem for all life. This manifests in never putting anyone down, not walking between conversing parties, not touching another's possession, not interrupting, speaking softly, genuinely listening, loving, and protecting all natural environments, honoring the religions of others, and never speaking unkindly of others (p. 76).
3. Honor for the tribal council. One may submit personal ideas to the council, but then must let go of any personal agenda and respect all other ideas. Once the council has reached consensus, one must never speak against group policy (p. 78).
4. One must be truthful at all times and under all conditions within the tribe (p. 78).
5. Show extraordinary hospitality, giving guests only your best food, accommodation, blankets, drink, and so on (p. 79).
6. One must empathize with others' feelings and know the spirit of the whole (p. 79).
7. One must receive strangers and outsiders with a loving heart and as members of the human family (p. 80).
8. All races are beautiful creations of the Creator, one family worthy of respect (p. 80).
9. Do not fill yourself with personal affairs, but remember the meaning of life is only known in serving others (p. 81).

**10.** Observe moderation and balance in all matters (p. 81).

**11.** Understand all that leads to personal well-being and all that leads to destruction (p. 81).

**12.** Follow the guidance given to one's heart, whether in dreams, prayer, solitude, or from wise elders and friends (p. 82).

Clearly, such an ethic has specific moral standards for communication. These include

**1.** listening fully with the heart, no matter how trivial or wrong the discussion may seem;

**2.** not interrupting another's communication;

**3.** not walking between conversants;

**4.** speaking softly, especially to elders;

**5.** speaking only by invitation when among a group of elders;

**6.** avoiding slander and defamation of all kinds;

**7.** communicating as an individual (contributing independent ideas to the council) first, then communicating in synch with the group (once policies have been set);

**8.** truth-telling;

**9.** *inner* communicating (morning and evening sanctification, periods of guidance) must precede outer communicating, openness to the Great Spirit is essential;

**10.** communicating with the whole tribe or whole earth in mind so as to honor others.

From this precise communication ethic may be drawn many other moral rules and principles. However, at the core of these ten (gentle) commandments is one guiding essence—respect. After conducting over two hundred interviews with Indigenous elders worldwide, I have learned that respect may be a universal attitude guiding many types of communication during peaceful times.

Such a cornerstone value is fundamentally different from the communication ethics of industrialized countries (Cooper 1989). When researching international communication ethics with a team of scholars from fourteen countries, Clifford Christians and I discovered that the leading values in Western communication codes of ethics are truthfulness, responsibility, and freedom, not respect. After analyzing hundreds of codes of ethics, we determined that the order of ethical values to which communication professionals aspire is (1) truthfulness (94 percent); (2) responsibility (92 percent); and (3) freedom (63 percent). However, codes are different from reality: the subscribers and viewers of most journalists, public relations staff, and entertainers worldwide often question whether such values are consistently applied. Moreover, *respect* is seldom mentioned as an important value.

While the authentic Native would honor these three values, especially truthfulness, she or he would bemoan the lack of emphasis on respect. For most Natives, respect would be the first value central to a communication "code." A primary means for such respect to be communicated is through silence, stillness, and inner listening. That the Western explorer often misinterpreted this silence as stupidity, aloofness, or hostility is tragic. Within some of the Salish schoolrooms I have visited, for example, non-Native teachers must still be warned not to chastise students for failing to immediately answer questions. This hesitancy is considered a sign of respect.

The Native communication ethic relies far more on personal demonstration than on mere lip-service. How one lives matters far more than what one says. In Eastern terms such a Native ethic reminds us of Ogaki Toyakota's dictum about the Shinto religion: "Shinto is a mode of practice more than of Scripture." In Western terms, Ralph Waldo Emerson's piercing comment seems akin to Indigenous philosophy: "Don't use words. Who you are stands above you and thunders so loudly all the while I can't hear a word you're saying." North American Natives abbreviate these dictums by simply commanding, "Walk your talk." In closed tribal societies, the individual's relative integrity is quickly perceived. Any preaching, or "talking without walking," will fall on deaf ears. Only when words echo years of morally disciplined living do they garner group interest.

## AUTHORITARIAN ETHICS

In many tribes, ethics is merely the collective mold imposed on the individual. Many Polynesian dances serve as a metaphor for this relationship: the dancer must precisely fit the group choreography; there is no space for individual improvisation, experimentation, or solo performance. It is as if the individual never dances or sings alone; each dancer is following the exact steps or notes of her predecessors. Such rigid orthodoxy seems apparent in Lawrence E. Sullivan's description of the Peruvian Incas, whose "ethical order is a prescribed experience of the world available in ritual. . . . Andean cosmogony appears to govern, through ritual, the structure of a community experience of that which is 'true' and 'real' (1989, 99). In some tribes, virtually every gesture, statement, and attitude is regulated by the tribe. An engaging, if sad, example occurs in Robert Gardner's film *Rivers of Sand,* in which a Hagar woman of Ethiopia reveals how her life is totally and typically molded by men. Images of her shackled feet and the molding of artifacts from metal accompany the dialogue.

## CROSS-CULTURAL INTERPRETATIONS

Before assuming that a "Native" ethic may be understood by Westerners, it is important to remember that research, like the individuals it reflects, is subjective and culture-bound. For example, the American Deborah Rose (1988) posits four principles of Australian Aboriginal morality: balance, symmetry, autonomy, and response. However, Les Hiatt, the Australian anthropologist, characterizes Aboriginal morality with four other dominant themes: fair play, anarchism, inalienability of land, and hospitality (interview, 9/21/90). Some Westernized Aboriginals might list other themes, while "purer" Aboriginals might state that such abstract lists are meaningless.

However, there is common ground. No matter which characterization of Aboriginal ethics is chosen, Captain James Cook (1728–1779), who first interacted with the Aboriginals, violated *all* Native ethics. He pitted guns against spears to violate fair play, seized "inalienable" land, met hospitality with the importation of disease and destruction, and replaced anarchy with domination. Balance, symmetry, and autonomy were supplanted by an uncomprehending colonial order. An organic ethic was emasculated by any organized ethic, one prescribed for Natives, but never personally implemented by Cook, who was eventually killed by Native Hawaiians.

## A COLLECTIVE ETHIC

In literate societies, a controversial ethical dilemma is often analyzed as a "case study," an isolated event needing close scrutiny. However, no tribal "case" is ever isolated. The individual has little personal identity in a collective world, as Pierre Bourdieu implies when discussing Kabyle (Mediterranean) society:

> *The point of honor is the basis of the moral code of an individual who sees himself always through the eyes of others, who has need of others for his existence, because the image he has of himself is indistinguishable from that presented to him*

*by other people. . . . [A]n insult sullies both the picture of*
*himself that the individual intends to project, and that which*
*he imagines to be his. (1966, 211)*

The high degree of intimate interaction in tribal society permits little isolation, even in thought about self. Much time is spent within the interplay of influence and imagining how one seems to others. Ethics in part are a means of managing appearances. For example, a Native American friend once told me, "You must bring tobacco to the elders before requesting an interview. This is not only a sign of respect but it keeps you from looking like an outsider."

Just as identity is inseparable from group feedback, so all behavior is interdependent. Given one's tribal role as part of the divine script, no movement could be isolated without affecting other actors, and even the Director (God). James E. Ritchie and Jane Ritchie allude to this organic cosmic and group cohesion when discussing Maori ethics:

*Breaches of etiquette or chiefly protocol did not merely have*
*social repercussions, but cosmic consequences as well. In the*
*wrong hands, or when uncontained and disorganized, every*
*vital power could diminish rather than enlarge human life.*
*(1989, 143)*

Thus the conscious Aboriginal felt a keen accountability for actions. Each movement affected community life and the spirit world, or divine order. It could not be amputated into a disconnected case study. Moreover, each action affected the land.

## A LAND ETHIC

Baird Callicott's "In Defense of the Land Ethic" (1989) implies that North American Indians were among the first and best environmentalists. Similarly, when the South American Cogi mountain dwellers granted their only interview to the outside world, their overarching ethic proved to be protection for the earth. For the reclusive Cogi of Peru, who were driven to the high Sierra by Spanish conquerors, ethics do not come from other humans but from the land itself. "The Great Mother taught us right and wrong. Now they are digging up the Mother's heart, and her eyes and ears. Stop digging and digging. Do not cut down trees—they hurt, like cutting off your own leg." (Eliare, 1990)

The Cogi's core ethic is simply "unless we do something, the world will end. If we act well, the world will not end." No philosophy could be simpler or call for greater human accountability. The Cogi surmise "if we act well, the earth will survive. If we do not, it will not" (Callicott 1989, 90). They hold this view in their smaller daily activities as well: "if crops aren't properly blessed, they dry up . . . that's how it is" (Eliare, 1990).

In this view there is no separation between a communication ethic and a land ethic. There are two priorities for Cogi communication: to bless the earth (and all its residents) and to warn of the earth's pending demise.

In the Native ethic, "communication" becomes a bond or covenant between earth and humans. There is no value in communication unless it is sacred and a blessing to the land. One Shuswap elder confided in me, "It is not just what the loud ghetto blasters do to us (who love the silence) which bothers me. What do these machines with hard, harsh sounds do to the gentle bird, the quiet tree, the soft-speaking earth?" In the Native ethic, communication must harmonize with its larger natural context.

From a larger perspective, the human is simply part of what the earth has "communicated" or created with the sacred Word or song. Possibly this is why Native languages had no original word for "communication"—what silences and sounds people originally expressed were inseparable from a larger ongoing creation. The Native notion of "communion" (and various synonyms) or natural harmony meant that one simply sang one's blending notes in the environmental chorus. Such sounds, like the healer's mantras, blessed the surrounding world and gave it health. To be ethical, to communicate ethically, to live by a land ethic were different names for the same integral process.

## SPECIALIZED ETHICAL INSTRUCTION

Three types of instruction have already been discussed. Children learned the first of these rules through observation, socialization (reward and punishment), and storytelling, such as the Alaskan Tlinglit's instructional tales about the mischievous Raven. In many societies, there were also more specialized forms of instruction, somewhat analogous to an intensive summer college workshop in ethics. Usually, such "advanced" sessions involved a rite of passage, "apprenticeship" into a leadership role, or collective preparation for a group activity. Tom Brown describes the learning period for an Apache shaman, Stalking Wolf:

> *Grandfather (Stalking Wolf) stayed in the lodge for six days of teaching from the elders. They all fasted; they all prayed. Sleep was rare. When one elder counseled Grandfather, the others would sleep. . . . He knew that this was his initiation to an apprenticeship in the shamanic way of life. . . . The lessons imparted during this session in the lodge formed the essentials of a code of ethics by which the healer and shaman lived, a*

*direction, and a path to greater spiritual power. Chant, song,*
*and ceremony followed each of the major lessons. (1988, 19)*

In *Moral Education Among the North American Indians,* Claude
Nichols describes how the Pima adolescent trained to follow in his
father's footsteps: "As he grew older his father required him to
listen to his lectures on the warrior and the citizen. Inattention
caused the father's stiffened middle finger to strike the boy's nose
and bring his head to the proper attitude" (1930, 32). In both
cases, Apache and Pima young men who received "advanced
training" could expect strict tutorials of focused intensity.

Possibly the most intensive training came in the "military
societies" of Native men. Like the Green Berets or the Queen's
Guard, these elite warriors privately banded together to promote
bravery in warfare. Just as at West Point, the oxymoronic notion
of "military ethics" (the moral way to kill, take captives, execute de-
serters, and address enemies) would be taught and reinforced.
Primarily, however, their function was to instill and underscore an
attitude of assurance and fortitude. Selfless martyrdom to the
tribe was the greatest value which was instilled since those in the
military societies faced a high mortality rate (Nichols 1930, 58–94).

Many ceremonies taught or involved ethical priorities. In the
Sundance, some "dancers" were suspended from poles by tethers
fastened to their lacerated chests. In addition to learning the
heroic endurance of pain, they learned integrity, fortitude, gen-
erosity, and bravery throughout the ritual. The discipline of
abstinence was simultaneously taught since dancers were
forbidden to communicate angrily, sexually, or impiously before,
during, and after the ceremonies (Nichols 1930, 58).

In specialized training, the adolescent might be taught a
gender-specific ethic. In many tribes, the male ethic was to provide, vigilantly protect, cautiously think, keep his word, endure

pain and suffering, be loyal to friends (until death), avenge wrong, and defend one's tribe and family. Conversely, the female ethic emphasized domestic industriousness, wise silence, cheerfulness, and provident nurturing.

Perhaps the subtlest ethical instruction came orally through aphorisms, sayings, oblique symbolism, and indirect implication. Often a youth might hear a phrase or see a symbol dozens of times before realizing its meaning. For example, the Maori phrase, "I will build my house from the lesser trees," had several implications not readily understood after a first listening. Depending on context, the phrase could mean "Remember the ordinary or little people," "Don't depend on the established order," or "Don't wait until you have what you think you want; work with what you have" (interview, Richie 1991). Each interpretation teaches an ethical value—humility, self-reliance, initiative—and yet the saying means more than the sum of these interpretations or values. Hence learning through oral innuendo was lifelong and on location. Only as one worked with one's hands and feet could the meanings of ethical folklore be discovered firsthand.

## CONFRONTING THE WHITE MAN'S ETHIC

Many stories are told about the intrusion and invasion of European communication practices and tools into the privacy of Native society. Reportedly cameras seemed to "steal the soul," and microphones "spooked the voice" of some innocent Aboriginals. In some societies, photographs inherently suggested black magic since any body part or likeness of a person could be used to place a curse on him or her. Moving pictures could "entrap" the spirit of a living person. Of a far more sinister nature, a dead person could be preserved on film, as if a haunting apparition had returned. Even the controversial gentle Tasaday "discovered" by

John Nance in the Philippines initially, "disliked the tape recorder" because it "[took] the voice of the Tasaday" (1975, 74).

Some of these "anti-media" stories now seem to be apocryphal or inflated for sensational effect. However, beneath the details of the true stories, and behind the essence of the others, rests a cultural conflict still in evidence. Because the Native was a "savage," "heathen," or "primitive man," he could be exported, exhibited, enslaved, and freely studied as a zoologist examines animals. Photographs, film, and tape recorders seemed to be instruments of control in such a context. Despite friendly exceptions, early introductions of media into Native society often seemed rapacious, part of a larger attempt to capture or seize Native culture for exportation and exploitation.

In many societies, women in nudist tribes were photographed by a man interested in more than their body paint. Films of authentic "Indians" were later edited into unflattering westerns, while documentaries about Africans bolstered the stereotypes epitomized in Tarzan and safari movies. Usually Indigenous People had no control, and often no knowledge, of how the new recording machines would depict them to large unknown populations.

Not only technology but imported Christian mores would conflict with local cultural norms. Although sexuality was highly regulated in many Indigenous societies, virtually all Natives felt monogamous or polygamous heterosexuality to be healthy. Christian ethics brought many forms of inhibition—Puritanism, Calvinism, Catholicism, and so on—that superimposed regulated fidelity, chastity, prudishness, and abstinence on Native "pagan" sexuality. Rather than proudly displaying their genitals, breasts, or fertility rites, most Native cultures began participating in a cover-up, an ethics of repression that led to wearing uncomfortable, hot clothing.

According to Ngapare Hopa, her Maori ancestors felt as if a vital life force, which was part of the natural order, was censored or neutered by the encroaching Western ethic (interview 1/15/91). Simultaneously, erotic and suggestive dances throughout the Americas and Africa were outlawed, sanitized, or exiled to more remote reservations.

In numerous countries many children were even taken from their parents and sent to missionary or state schools that forbade Native customs and languages. "Sterilized," "castrated," "muzzled," "muted," "emasculated," "dehumanized," "censored," "censured," "Victorianized," and "domesticated" are just a few of the adjectives that educated Aboriginals later used to describe how the imported ethic suffocated the natural one. In one former student's words, "When your language is forbidden, your culture denied, your true feelings forever suppressed, you become the walking dead... your communication is pasted upon you by outsiders... you speak English, but think Carrier; you dress Canadian, but feel Indian; outside you live by the rules, but inside you die by the minute" (anonymous interview 4/12/91).

Summarily imported technologies, theologies, and pedagogies seemed to suffocate the life force of Indigenous society. Natural rhythms were forced toward artificial technology . . . and the Gods were silenced. Rape, a common practice of conquering soldiers, also became a convincing metaphor for a conquering culture violently dominating Native societies.

## HONORING NATIVE LANGUAGE AND PERSPECTIVE

"Communication ethics" are two words most Native languages would never have included. The language of each society is unique. Views of morality and of the stigmas attached to breaches of morality are embedded in the syntax and vocabulary of each language. Some languages may have a different word for every crime or law; others cluster related transgressions into a single concept.

As an example of linguistic influence, consider this comparison. In English, matters of communication ethics are usually divided by category. Matters of defamation of character (attacks on reputation), for example, are usually divided into two categories, slander (oral defamation) and libel (printed defamation). By contrast, consider Native Hawaiian cultural interpreter David Malo's discussion of the subtler distinctions created in the Hawaiian language:

> If a person seeks to find fault with another, there are many ways of doing it, the chief of which is slander (aki-biting), defamation (ahi-ahi), making false accusations (niania), circulating slanders (holoholooleo), vilifying (makaulii), detraction (kaamehai), belittling (kuene), tale-bearing (poupou-noho-ino), ensnaring (hoowale-wale), misleading (luahele), treachery (ku-makaia), fault-finding (hooleue-hala), malice (opuinoino), scandal-mongering (law-olelo-wale), reviling (paonioni), and a host of other things. (1960, 73)

Each of these words and the subtle shadings of meanings implied by their differences reminds us that ethical notions are particular, linguistic, and tribal, not just generic or universal.

Similarly, *attitudes* toward communication ethics are ethnic- or culture-specific. For example, the European and the Native American might disapprove of lying but adopt differing attitudes toward prevaricators. For the European, lying was a violation of Scripture and of "the Truth" revered in the Christian New Testament. For the Native, "lying" might signify insanity: one who did not speak truth surely must not know what it is and therefore must have lost touch with reality. Thus cultural attitudes would differ: the white man who lied was devious, deceitful and not to be trusted by his fellows; however, within some tribes, the Native who lied was simply to be pitied, if not to be treated for his mind disease.

Priorities often differ across cultures. The greatest communication offense in many societies was to insult the gods. In others, it was to insult the chief. In still others, it was merely to utter kapu words. In Rubellite Johnson's Kawaii, the greatest insult possible was for a rival to capture and spit on one's bones (interview 1/15/91). It was equally reprehensible to use or abuse another person's name, a matter closely akin to our worst form of slander. In some societies, insults violating communication ethics were so unwelcome, some were punished by torture, exile, or death.

What is often forgotten, however, is that most Native societies had a *positive* communication ethic. The "kapu" or "tapu" (taboo) list of "thou shalt nots" was counterbalanced by a stronger sense of what *should* or *could* be expressed. As in some Western cultures, many "thou shalts" included numerous forms of uplifting and fulfilling forms of communication—dancing, singing, chanting, worship, silence, praise, thanksgiving, and humor. Indeed, within some island lore, it is said that the ocean waves once blended harmoniously with the waves of human laughter.

## Summary

Whether perceived as rules, laws, or ethics, Native regulation of communication was traditional and specific. With minor exceptions, communication rules were passed on from generation to generation in the home and, in the case of tribal elites, by advanced specialized training sessions and ceremonies. The detailed ethical rules (ethics) of society derived from a larger ethic that dictated the life of the group, the individual, and nature itself.

Communication ethics varied according to gender, rank, age, and tribe. Particular language, locale, and attitude influenced local communication laws and other rules. However, a universal tribal ethic may be outlined which emphasized respect as the core value of Native communication.

An encroaching European communication ethic, which emphasized broken rules and invasive communication tools, was imposed on Indigenous People who preferred stillness, truth-telling, and the natural order. Despite this conflict in cultures, and the resulting sterilization of Native life, traces of an authentic communication may still be found in Aboriginal expression. This positive communication ethic is especially preserved in dance, music, art, storytelling, ceremony, and humor.

To be sure, exceptions prove the rule of many patterns reported above. Many tribes developed a different communication ethic for speaking to rivals, colleagues, outsiders, and enemies. Similarly, not all Europeans lacked compassion or stereotyped Indigenous communication practices. Nor were all settlers narrow-minded; some saw it as valuable to be bilingual and bicultural, as did some Indigenous chiefs, scouts, and scholars. Indeed, one seldom noted communication achievement of the Indigenous thinker was his eventual mastery and use of English, Spanish, and other languages by which to negotiate with the conqueror.

Consequently, generalizations about universal Indigenous communication are limited and filled with exceptions. After various global parallels have been noted, it is important to inspect each People case by case. Such is the purpose of each of the next two chapters, which delineate the communication practices of the Shuswap people of British Columbia and the Navajo people of Arizona.

# CHAPTER FIVE

*These Northwest Coast petroglyphs are located between the high and low tides, probably to communicate directly with the underwater Salmon People. Bones of the salmon are thrown back into the water, so the fish can be reborn and will feed the people. Drawing © by Sabra Moore.*

# The Shuswap People of British Columbia: A Case Study

So far this book has presented a *general* overview of indigenous communication illustrated by specific examples. Both for balance and depth it is useful to turn this process around and inspect *specific* tribes and practices.

In chapters 5 and 6, I turn to specific Western scholarly methods: the field study, case study, and interview techniques are blended to report on the communication and ethics of two significantly different peoples, the Shuswap of British Columbia (Canada) and the Navajo people (Diné) of Arizona (U.S.A.).

I selected specific Navajo and Shuswap groups to ask about the "old ways" of communicating for many reasons. They were distinctive Native nations, one living in the arid semidesert interior of the United States, the other living in frozen, forested, water-filled coastal Canada. Each had its own oral history with distinctive myth, lore, and spirit. Both were groups I greatly respected due to their ancient artistry, industry, and integrity. Of great practical importance, both were communities where I could visit as less of an "outsider" since close friends were respected "sisters" who lived in or near the reserves. From all I could determine, both Native nations also had unique approaches to communication.

In the winter of 1991 I set out for central British Columbia to pose questions to two bands of Shuswap Natives living on "re-serves," the term Canadians use rather than "reservations." I traveled by train and bus hundreds of miles north of populous areas like Vancouver and Seattle. My friend Dorothy Hughes who lived in 100 Mile House, a town situated between the Canim Lake and Alkali Lake Shuswap bands, introduced me to her old friends at these two Shuswap reserves. During the spring and early summer I visited and occasionally lived at the reserves, situated perhaps one hundred miles apart, and interviewed elders and other community leaders.

Two questions motivated my research: "What were the early forms and ethical rules of Shuswap communication?" and "What might we (modern non-Shuswap observers) learn from these earlier customs and ethics?"

This chapter will inspect three questions in the following order:

1. Who were and are the Shuswap?
2. What were their traditional forms of communication?
3. What rules governed their customary communication?

Other questions such as "What may we learn from this approach to communication?" will be discussed in the final chapter.

My own ethics were scrutinized in this process. Was I, like many researchers, simply trying to take valuable information from a Native group, or was I willing to give in return? At their request, I was happy to give talks, to teach band members to conduct research themselves, to give a workshop, to participate in the local culture (sweat houses, ceremonial singing and dancing, building and sleeping in a tepee, etc.), to copyright and share my research for local use, and to videotape then donate interviews with specific elders for the tribe's archives. I was also delighted to donate toward scholarships for young Natives and provide other gifts without being nudged—to me it seemed valuable to participate openly in the community as a friend and equal based on the Shuswap values of respect and reciprocity, not to import foreign values and a hidden agenda.

## Who Are the Shuswap?

From an outsider's perspective, one means of understanding Native Peoples has been by language classification. The "Salish" language group of Indians included many different tribes and bands dispersed throughout (what are now) the Canadian Southwest and American Northwest. The largest Native "nation" (i.e., conclave, people) in central British Columbia was called the "interior Salish," since the various tribes spoke similar "Salishan" languages.

These interior Salish people consisted of five tribes who were at various times friendly or hostile to one another—the Lilloett, the Okenagan, the Thompson, the Lake, and the Shuswap Indians. Interior Salish groups differed in customs, dialects, and even physical appearance from the Salishan-speaking Indians of the coast (Jenness 1977, 351) and the southern interior.

Within southern central British Columbia the Shuswap "controlled the Fraser River Valley from Lilloett to Alexandria and all the country eastward to the summits of the Rocky Mountains" (Jenness 1977, 351). Having dwindled to perhaps 6,000 full-blooded people by this century, the Shuswap probably numbered more than 15,000 in 1780 when European settlers and trappers began to influence Western Natives (Jenness 1977, 359). More conservative estimates by Barbara Leitch (1975) suggest only 4,000 Shuswap people had survived by the late 1970s. During the last century they had decreased from twenty-nine to eighteen bands. These eighteen bands were assigned 146,000 acres of reserve land in British Columbia, including land near Canim Lake and Alkali Lake, the two reserves chosen for this research.

The earliest written records about the Shuswap come from white explorers and traders and thus often bore the astigmatic distortions of first impressions by cultural outsiders. Catherine Brow (1967) cites the early explorations of Franz Boas (1891), James Dawson (1981), and particularly James Teit (1904, 1909) as giving the most extensive outsider's view of Shuswap culture, during a period when Natives were first assimilated, often arbitrarily and artificially, into Western society. Although settlers had met the Shuswap as early as the 1700s, little relevant writing has survived. Moreover, later studies (e.g., Atrigg 1964, and Rogers 1970) seem either more interested in the modern Shuswap or largely derivative of the earlier materials.

To the Shuswap people history is only recently enmeshed with the white foreigners who surprisingly appeared in the 1700s. Long before, their history and cosmology began with a great Force or Being, known as the Old One:

> *He traveled the land creating the mountains, streams, everything. He left, but the task of creating the world was not complete. The Old One sent his helper, Coyote, to make it right. Coyote had many encounters with plants, animals, and people. Each time, the world was changed, making it a better place to live. (Coffey et al. 1990, 7)*

To the Shuswap such stories were no more "myth" than Genesis is to the devout Jew or Christian or the big bang theory and the theory of evolution are to scientists. Indeed many Shuswap "legends" show a sensitivity to natural ecology, botany, zoology, and geology that makes their origins an integral part of natural, not social, history.

Sadly, from the Shuswap perspective, the white man's role in this natural history is the opposite of the Old One's "creation"—an almost perpetual destruction and antisocial, antinatural history. In 1858 the gold rush brought an influx of often-insensitive prospectors who routinely claimed Native land and evicted the natural inhabitants. More devastating were the epidemics imported by Europeans which decimated over 70 percent of the Shuswap population between 1850 and 1903 (Coffey et al. 1990, 35). Indeed, if Canadian Indian Department figures were accurate, eleven entire Shuswap bands were eliminated during the late 1800s by the influx of smallpox, pneumonia, and other imported diseases.

Regrettably, most memory of the early Shuswap died with these previous generations and with bands now extinct. However, relevant surviving oral history of the people themselves will be presented here. Written histories of the Shuswap by Native authors are now appearing. Good examples are *Shuswap History: The First Hundred Years of Contact* by J. Coffey et al. (1990) and *The Shuswap: One People With One Mind, One Heart, and One Spirit* by the Shuswap National Tribal Council (1989).

As there were no known Native accounts of the Shuswap written prior to World War I, James Teit's *The Shuswap* is the most authentic and reliable written account of that era for many reasons. Teit's travels over a ten-year period brought him to live in or visit virtually all of the Shuswap bands. He was married to a Thompson Indian (Brow 1967). He was empathetic and open-minded about being educated by Native perspectives. He was a trained member of the larger Jesup North Pacific Expedition supervised by Dr. Franz Boaz; Teit took painstaking notes and made careful drawings with a scientist's eye for accuracy. He had visited and befriended many other Native bands so he could view the Shuswap not only from distant and interior perspectives but also from the immediately adjacent vantage points of many long-term Shuswap neighbors. Finally, Teit's is the only comprehensive text prior to the erosion of authentic Shuswap practices of the nineteenth century.

The Shuswap bands Teit found were salmon fishers and hunters of deer, elk, porcupine, marmot, beaver, and other game. Supplementing their diet with roots and berries, they also used plants and liquids in healing practices. Migratory by season, they built temporary dwellings such as hunting, fishing, girls' and women's lodges, and also more permanent dwellings such as partly subterranean lodges (with ladders and smoke holes) that protected against long winters. In times of peace they enjoyed numerous games from lacrosse to ring and hoop. In times of war they formed attack parties and were frequently raided by neighboring rivals.

Teit thought the Shuswap were divided into classes—chiefs, nobles, commoners, and slaves. They had celebrated the potlatch ceremonies until the late nineteenth century. Although each band had already been given arbitrary boundaries as established by the Indian Department, they still practiced shamanism, storytelling, tattooing of wrists, face painting, and other traditional customs.

Overall, Teit found the Shuswap laudatory, including their reputation among surrounding tribes. They seemed the best basket-makers, more open to new approaches, affectionate and indulgent to children, hospitable and friendly to strangers, coura-geous, stable, and tenacious of purpose. He quoted Simon Fraser's observation of 1808 that the "Shuswap were more honest than any other tribe on this side of the mountains" (Teit 1909, 470).

Although unable to pin down any one meaning for the word "Shuswap," Teit did trace its etymology to a white corruption of Native words and found that "Shuswaps" had been called many other names by other bands, including "Atnas" or "foreigner." Just as the name itself had evolved, so, too, had Shuswap bands, which were products of migrations, intermarriage, conflicts, and dynamic offshoots from other tribes.

An enduring people, the Shuswap encountered winters as low as -70° F and summers too short for major agriculture. Their extended families often clustered three or four generations within a single lodge. Expeditions for hunting and rites of passage in the mountains or woods could be dangerous, so much daily activity and training were geared toward survival.

Compiling statistics, Teit showed the devastating effects of the smallpox, influenza, and other epidemics. Although the Alkali Lake band had only decreased from 175 in 1850 to 172 in 1906, the Canim Lake band had shrunk from 350 people to 77 over the same period. Deep scars were inflicted on the memory of the Shuswap people by the encroachment of European settlers, scars still present a century later.

Essentially peaceful and often playful, the Shuswap engaged in protective and occasionally assertive battle. Sharing many language characteristics with their neighbors, they engaged in intertribal trade, marriage, and potlatch. Although relatively poor materially, they were considered rich in the quality of their arts, hunting, storytelling, birch bark canoe building, and family life.

## Shuswap Communication

*. . . they used to paint themselves bright red, used to smash it (the powder rock) up, dilute it and paint themselves for war, for celebrations, for what all . . . and the chief's face and hands would be painted bright red. —Shuswap Elder "Augusta"* from The Days of Augusta. *(Speare 1977, 69)*

The red paint came from what Teit took to be "micaceous hermanite [*sic*], giving a reddish sparkling color . . . used for decorating bows and arrows, and as facial paint" (Teit 1909, 475). Wolf moss, used for painting the skin, and many other dyes and colors were employed.

Each color and stroke had a meaning, referring to a spirit or animal, to one's guardian species or temperament. As Shuswap elder Augusta remembered, paint was worn not for war per se, but at rituals and ceremonies rich with symbolic meaning, which included war, its preparation, and honoring its casualties.

Sign language was equally specific. Used more as an intertribal go-between language than within tribes (in which a common language was spoken), Shuswap hand signs had value for intertribal greetings, negotiations, happenstance hunting meetings, and warnings. As late as 1904, Teit identified over one hundred Salish hand signs.

A Shuswap shaman (physician and spiritual leader) might "communicate" in any or all of the following ways: incantation, massaging body parts, sprinkling water on the head, singing, speaking specific phrases, prescribing, laying on of hands, blowing water on the body, sucking evil spirits away, assisting souls to enter heads, transplanting spirits, performing with masks and instruments, exorcising disease, and repeating healing gestures (Leitch 1975, 432; Teit 1909, 615; Palmer 1980, 1).

It was said by the elders' elders that a competent tracker could hear a feather drop, could distinguish twenty bird calls, and could listen for the "absence" of sound. When the wind stopped, when the animals were quiet, when the owl suddenly fell silent—these "absences" could be "heard." In essence, Shuswap listening was amplified and focused, like powerful radar.

Similarly, a leader might be chosen for his power of speech (Danaher 1990, 20), and speaking was important for storytelling, advising, discussion of community affairs, prayer, and chant. Cleverness or insight in speaking carried some weight, but the

actual power and authority of voice, grounded in a strong presence, genuineness, and assurance, seemed to make the speech
and the speaker more capable of magic and leadership.

> "Super-natural" encounters often involved guardian spirits:
> . . . each Shuswap child trained alone in the hills to receive a
> "guardian spirit" or "power." The guardian spirit guided and
> protected the young person and bestowed special skills or
> (super-natural) strength and vision. The close relationship
> between a person and his or her own spirit power dominated
> Shuswap religious thought. Every year this relationship was
> renewed during the winter ceremonials when each person
> sang and danced to imitate his own power. (Bouchard and
> Kennedy 1979, iv)

An entire new range of communication opened to the child in
finding his or her power. The child would commune with a greater
force, summon it as needed, and discover an essence of self to
express in many other communication forms: "After the boy had
found his power and his own special song, he returned to the
village. . . . [S]ometimes the boy would paint a picture of his
power on a rock cliff. . . . [M]y great-grandfather's power was a
rock (Ike Willard, quoted in Bouchard and Kennedy 1979, 127).

Hence the Shuswap girl and boy learned not only to communicate with a special being (or "species" to the outsider) but
also to then use every major art form—dance, painting, song,
speech—to portray and present that Being. While many interpreters of the culture feel more comfortable saying these early
Natives "imitated" their force, the elders' memory suggests that,
when dancing or singing, they "became" or "took on" their
guardian spirit—an extremely intense and paranormal communication form in modern terms.

Preparing to become a Shuswap doctor also meant changing

modes of communication. As George Pete explained, "Up the highest mountains around the village . . . you had to rise early in the morning and bathe in spring water . . . have sweats, meditate, and pray every day to the Great Spirit . . . and most important of all, when the big day comes for you to receive your Power, which will happen in the sweat, you must not be afraid of the spirit or you will never receive your powers" (Canim Lake/Gonzaga 1991, 11). Pete tells of the importance of inner communication. Fear prevents the receiving of a powerful signal; openness invites the transmission to be received.

In all these rites of passage an individual prepared for a different level of communication, transcended the ordinary forms, and augmented the repertoire of expressive skills found within the society. An experience of aloneness and remoteness from daily surroundings was essential to find this "new voice." Like the adolescent male voice change, the identity change included a transition in communication.

Silence was revered by earlier generations of Shuswap. Practical information, such as the sounds of approaching animals or weather patterns, could be perceived. However, silence was also a spiritual necessity, so that the presence of the Great Spirit and lesser Entities could be sensed and proper respect shown for the many creations of the Old One and Coyote. Early settlers thought (and some recent non-Shuswap contacts still think) that long silences in response to questions were evidence of retardation or antisocial reaction. On the contrary, silence breaks purposefully punctuated conversation to allow for careful thinking, to show respect for the speaker, and to honor the tempos of nature.

Both Canim Lake and Alkali Lake elders, such as Laura Harry, Amelia Johnson, Rita Charlie, and Jim Frank, remembered early communication networks among the Shuswap. Horseback riders or runners, who lived in adjacent valleys or neighboring communities, would bring messages of important events (deaths, battles, weddings, special ceremonies) from tribe to tribe in a relay manner. When an impassable river or mountain might delay the message, a fire would be built and puffs of smoke, caused by covering the fire briefly with animal hides, would transmit a simplified version of the message.

In essence, all transportation was also communication. Johnny Johnson of Alkali Lake reflected, "You would learn to follow the water like a blood vein in the ground—it would tell you something by its direction; as you moved about you would communicate with the land, follow the animals. . . . It was all a part of you. . . . The elders knew intuitively where everything was." Mark Boyce of Canim Lake remembered this similar intercourse with the land's language and spoke poetically of "talking to rocks," "taking on a bird's traits," and hunting by learning to cooperate with nature's signals.

Speaking with animals was not a generic, lump-sum activity. Each species was unique—could teach you, warn you, or bring news—depending on its nature and yours. The owl (or "Owl") was most frequently mentioned as a harbinger of death. If Owl spoke to you in the Shuswap language, it might tell you who had died, but just as likely it would caution that some unidentified person in your band had already or would soon pass away.

Canim Lake former Chief Charlotte Christopher recalled being with a group of five people when the "Owl spoke to us in Shuswap and said we should return home." Alkali Lake educator Fred Johnson said that Owl was the most feared in many tribes because it always brought bad news that could directly affect you and your family.

The Beaver's communication was equally specialized and more intriguing. Canim Lake educator Elizabeth Pete explained, "after you killed it and opened it up, you could 'read' the beaver's *sk'ulem* (spleen). This organ, by its shape told you something for the beaver—it might tell you how well your trapping would go, or might forecast the weather, or might tell you were going to forget something."

Canim Lake elder Dora Archie, band administrator Alana Dixon, and band member Fred Christopher confirmed Beaver's ability to tell the future.

Communication with, not merely from, animals was appropriate. A local community paper, The Tribune, confirmed in Felix Archie's obituary (June 5, 1980) that Felix "spoke to the bear" to tell it "that he did not want to kill him." It was common practice to apologize or explain to an animal the reason for its impending death. This practice was part of a larger reverence for all life—as elder Ike Daniels commented: "If you didn't respect an animal, then you couldn't kill any more of its kind . . . and you certainly wouldn't kill it unless you needed it for food or clothing or something for survival."

Most elders painted a different picture than the utopian vision that all animals spoke and were affectionate. Alkali elder Ellen Robbins noted, "You had to work hard at breaking through to many animals . . . it was hard work." Elder May Dixon noted, "It took a real long time for Coyote to trust you. For trust to be established, many animals would study Natives from a distance for weeks or years before risking intimacy."

Sound was not necessary for an animal to emit messages. The very presence of Hawk or Eagle was a positive omen, just as a two-headed snake was negative. An unexpected visit from your guardian spirit could be an epiphanic moment.

Communion was with all of life. Each tree was a living spirit and could speak if one were patient and wise enough to hear it. Alkali Lake elder Lily Squinahan remembered, "They could talk to the trees—or tell them their troubles . . . like a confession." To cut down a tree without its permission or without a need for the wood from the entire tree was sacrilege.

Alive and sentient, rocks could be addressed but not moved without permission. Since the landscape was part of an organic whole, to move a stone or dig a pit without consent would be like transplanting a human lung or cutting into a person's leg. With patience, one could observe a totally different type of communication as part of the natural world, rather than a part from it.

As Freddy Johnson articulated,

*They saw all as Divine. Just like you, all of nature could be hurt. Everything is your Teacher—the mountain, the water, the wind, the rocks are your Teacher. Because they are so old, the rocks and the water are your Grandfather and Grandmother. . . . What is freshly alive is your Brother and Sister . . . like a tree or bird.*

Such a feeling of a family of life led to a finer level of observation of interspecies communication, such as "when the sunlight first hit the trees, they started praying" (F. Johnson), and "just as the rain cleanses its brother the grass, so it cleanses your words in the air when it comes down" (J. Johnson). These friends and family would also help you—the stars, clouds, moon, leaves, earth, and sky all told direction, changes in season, weather, and the Great Spirit's plan.

For each Shuswap man and woman, direct communion with the Great Spirit was an apex experience. Mary Alice Danaher, director of Canim Lake's Gonzaga College program and respected honorary band member, noted, "One communicated with the Great Spirit with the greatest of respect. One had an overwhelming sense of the Great Spirit's presence, protection, and the responsibility to ask its permission to use this world."

Elders of both communities pointed out a variety of forms

for contacting the Great Spirit: (1) praying out loud in Shuswap; (2) going up into the mountains to meditate; (3) being close to the shaman, who would make contact; (4) contacting the sacred soul in one's self; 5) participating in the pipe ceremony with an attitude of worship; (6) attending the ceremonial sweat lodge ceremony; and (7) participating in ceremonial dancing, singing, powwows, and other group sacred events. Given the many unique and important cultural features of the final three types of group communication—the pipe, sweat, and social ceremonies— each will be given more detailed elaboration. The Alkali Lake band has revived and imported these traditional events and elevated them to a central place within band activity. While the Canim Lake band seems more interested in these activities to preserve and understand their roots, they maintain sweat lodge activities, pass the talking stick, and travel freely to cultural events at other reserves.

## THE PIPE CEREMONY

Of the many group communication activities, the pipe ceremony may be best known. Usually thought of as the "peace pipe" by outsiders (since they encountered it at treaty negotiation events), the wooden carved pipe was smoked long before treaty "peace" settlements with settlers. The tobacco leaf within the pipe was sacred, produced a mild spiritual expansion when inhaled, and produced a spiraling smoke that ascended through the lodge or tepee "skylight," as if to the Great Spirit. Since such dwellings were often confined to minimal ventilation, the smoke could also linger and produce a form of incense. At the heart of the ceremony were prayers, stories, and thoughts, which allowed those participating to transcend daily events and collectively connect with a higher power.

## THE SWEAT LODGE CEREMONY

In some bands, the pipe ceremony was incorporated into the hot sweat lodge ceremonies. A sweat lodge was an igloo-shaped sauna made of animal hides stretched across a wooden frame. Participants in the sweat lodge wore little if any clothing and sweated heavily from the 300°F temperatures produced by heated lava rocks. Within an intimate, roasting atmosphere, men (and sometimes women, who had separate sweat lodges) participated in a variety of ceremonies that included some combination of these elements: singing in unison, the pipe ceremony, telling stories, structured alternation of chanting or singing by fixed numbers of singers, adding specific numbers of heated rocks to the center of the lodge floor, ritual prayer or speaking to the Great Spirit, alternate singing by soloist and group, group silence, and variations on these forms.

These sweats, such as the Grandmother Ceremonial Sweat, were more formal than the social "cleansing" sweats. Although the format changed from band to band, generally the ceremonial sweats restricted casual entering and exiting of the lodge during ceremonies, whereas the cleansing sweats were more first-come, first-served style, like a steam room or public sauna. In the cleansing sweats, one might stay any length of time, tell jokes, laugh, discuss casual matters, and come and go on impulse for a swim or bath. At the heart of both types of sweats, which varied in format from tribe to tribe, was a personal process of purification. As Mary-Anne Archie described it, "My muscles and body begin to relax in the steaming bath. . . . I can sense the release of any emotional feeling within me. My mind acknowledges the peace around me and soothes my mood . . . I begin to . . . cleanse myself" (Canim Lake/Gonzaga, 5). As body toxins were secreted through the skin pores, the individual had the sensation of lightening, unwinding, and opening consciousness to a higher power.

A variety of larger ceremonies—most of which included singing, dancing, and instruments—were commonplace among the Shuswap. As E. S. Rogers observed, "Summer was a time for religious festivals and dances. They might also be held in winter. The songs sung at the dances had been obtained from the spirit world and the ceremonies held to bring the souls of the dead back to life and initiate a time of abundance and ease" (Rogers 1970, 59).

## THE POWWOW

Powwows were one form of social gathering in which festival dances and singing could be shared. According to Ann Theodore of the Canim Lake/Gonzaga band, the traditional powwow featured most or all of these elements: the hosting and feeding of traveling guests, a grand entry in which all dancers were ceremonially dressed, all-day (and sometimes all-night) dancing, guest speakers who discussed the culture and their beliefs, competitions among dancers. Elders noted a wide variety of other elements present in some powwows—drum playing, dancing by all present, blessing the infants, an address by the chief, the pipe ceremony, games, and prayers.

## SPECIAL DANCES

Some of the special dances had unique ritual functions. Diamond Jenness noted the Ghost or Circle Dance practiced in summer or winter "whenever some member of a band claimed to have received a message from the land of ghosts" (1977, 357). Teit had heard of, if not witnessed, the Hunger Dance, featuring a naked man painted as a skeleton, and noted many of the animal imitation dances, among them salmon, caribou, and moose (1909, 584).

Elder Ike Willard described a version of the animal imitation dance ceremony. Following a particular sequence (below), the evening (or in some cases, the weeklong) ceremony might include these ordered components:

1. the host beat the drum;
2. the host started the dance;
3. old people sang;
4. everyone could then join in;
5. the host spoke to people about right and wrong;
6. old people gave speeches about the secret of their longevity;
7. one person announced his song—of a specific animal and power;
8. he or she then sang solo;
9. others joined in;
10. he or she then danced imitating or "becoming" the animal whose song was sung.

These movements of imitation were called the s-tlai dance (Willard, in Bouchard and Kennedy 1979, 129).

## THE POTLATCH CEREMONY

Often such dances, songs, pipe ceremonies, and celebrations were part of a large potlatch ceremony. A major hospitality event, the potlatch featured the celebrating of an important occasion such as a birth, coming of age, death, a new title, a new name, or marriage. Essential to the potlatch was a specialized form of gift-giving. One gift was the provision of food for as many as several hundred people for several weeks, prepared by the host family. More particular gifts were offered to specific guests and records were made of what was given to whom. Paid witnesses observed the gift-giving since a recipient of a gift would be expected to "pay it back with interest" later (Hawthorn 1957, 69).

Shuswap people of the Lake district (including Canim Lake and Alkali Lake) gathered every year at Green Lake, "the Great Gathering Place," in large numbers. Mary Alice Danaher noted that "goods were bartered, trout were trapped, games were played, and sports of all kinds were enjoyed. The people feasted, danced, and told stories" (1990, 18). The gathering was an annual social climax anticipated for many moons (months).

## THE DRUM

Core experiences of such group communication were a deepening sense of community and worship. At the center of the dance and music was a symbol of the earth's heartbeat, the drum. Indeed, the drum was often referred to as "the heartbeat." Whether played by a solo drummer or a circle of drummers, the drum was carefully handcrafted for endurance and sonic penetration.

## LANGUAGE

Invisibly central to singing, chanting, and speaking was the Shuswap language, Shikwatmuk. Derivative of what was possibly one unified Salish language two thousand years ago, it is now one of the four branches of Northern Interior Salish (lecture, Mandy Jimmy 5/11/91). Without the concepts of verbs and nouns, as perceived in English, and other major structural differences, the language proceeded from and produced a substantially different mindset. For example, Shuswap stories, which feature the entertaining trickster Coyote, are often hilarious when told in Shuswap, but only mildly amusing, if funny at all, when translated into English.

Naming of people and objects carried special power to the early Shuswap. Each part of the land—whether valley, mountain, or woods—had a sacred name. People took on names that brought out essences of their nature, unlike their more mundane, imposed Anglo-Saxon names. Naming ceremonies held special significance since the assuming of a new name, like a new title, could be viewed as growth in character or position, or the more precise locating and uttering of one's sacred identity.

Canim Lake elder Ike Daniels said, "God is in everything; be careful how you use it." An expansion of his dictum seemed central to early Shuswap communication—"God is in everything; be careful how you name it"; "God is in everything; be careful how you speak to it"; "God is in everything; be careful how to thank Him." Thankfulness to the Great Spirit—for harvest, for rain, for life itself, and for every major event—was central to Shuswap ceremony.

All communication evolved out of an awareness of the animated, spiritual nature of all forms. Some forms, like the pipe ceremony and smoke signals, were shared with many other Indigenous People. Other forms, such as language and particular sweat ceremonies, were either regional or entirely unique.

Since silence, stillness, listening, and relating to all life forms were key elements of Shuswap communication, it seems more accurate to call the earlier forms communion, not communication. Words and images grew out of a shared reality and context, not from abstractions or a need for isolated "information." Moreover, beneath all communication was nature's rhythm. That rhythm had first to be acknowledged and tuned in before messages could be sent.

Intuitively, each person had to sense a flow or pulse of nature that came from observation, profound listening, and inner discernment. To blurt out words without significance or practical necessity was a sign of weakness or insanity. Only communion was sane, safe, and substantial.

## Shuswap Communication Ethics

According to Coffey and his colleagues, "The Shuswap 'ethic' emphasized stewardship. They lived in harmony with the land, using nature in a way which would not result in damage to the environment. Respect for the land was shown through conservation. Birch bark was only taken in the spring, when the outer bark could be removed without killing a tree. When animals were taken for food and clothing, nothing was wasted" (1990, 7). A primary value within this ethic was natural freedom—for animals and plants to grow and for people to roam the land. That this freedom has been lost is summarized in the words of elder Cecelia Bob: "Now, most of our hunting grounds are fenced in and post 'No trespassing' . . . there's no freedom around the place like we had before" (interview, 1991 in Dawson, G2).

Alongside stewardship and freedom was an ethic of sharing. When prospectors invaded the Caribou country during the gold rush, Natives were shocked by the notion of "claims," as if property could be owned by an individual. Shuswap bands had always cooperatively lived on land that belonged ultimately to the Great Spirit. Undergirding this land ethic were values outlined by Wilma Christopher. In her view, the Shuswap felt linked together belonging to the Earth, respect for the power the Earth holds in supporting all living things, respect for what is taken from the Earth, an innate responsibility to help each other (Canim/ Gonzaga 1991, 5).

Antoine Archie underscored the ethic of individual responsibility that grew naturally from such values. For example, in the field of child rearing, "when elders saw children carrying on and

misbehaving they would say: 'that child does not have parents'"
(Canim/Gonzaga 1990, 5). A parent was expected to train a child
firmly through example and discipline. Responsibility for all one
brought into the Earth and took from the Earth was mandatory.

It is not surprising that after the infusion of Christian religions,
the Shuswap became sandwiched between two ethical systems:

> *The missionaries had the most drastic effect on the Shuswaps.*
> *In 1842, Father Desmet met the Shuswap people for the first*
> *time. The goal of the missionaries was to convert the Indian*
> *people to Christianity and a European way of life—to 'civilize.'*
> *They didn't understand that the Shuswaps held beliefs that*
> *provided a harmonious life. Instead, they believed that they*
> *could force Indian children to adopt a totally new and foreign*
> *way of living. By the turn of the century, several residential*
> *schools were built. Children were forced to attend and on*
> *threat of punishment, had to adopt the British customs and*
> *language. (Coffey et al. 1990, 8)*

The Shuswap soon discovered themselves bound between two
legal systems as well:

> *The Indians had their own system of justice, dispensed by the*
> *chiefs. With the arrival of the traders, there were now two sets*
> *of laws: traditional Indian law and Hudson's Bay Company*
> *law. Inevitably, there was conflict between the two. The*
> *Hudson's Bay attempted to impose its system of justice on the*
> *Indians. Hudson's Bay policy required that Indians who in-*
> *jured traders, or their property, be tried under European law.*
> *Penalties were often severe. However, this policy did not apply*
> *in cases of an Indian injuring another Indian. Nor did it*
> *apply if a trader injured an Indian. (Coffey et al. 1990, 16)*

This double standard, of treating whites with one system of justice and Natives with another, was also at odds with the Shuswap ethic. Ultimately, however, for self-protection, Natives learned to initiate the seemingly unfair white ethic with two standards. Like most Natives, the Shuswap developed a double ethic as well: they mandated truth-telling among themselves but learned to deceive the "white man" (and rival tribes or suspect visitors) or deliberately withhold information. To tell where the better hunting grounds were meant losing the best game to white settlers. To tell which herbs were best for curing diseases meant having to buy back medicines made of these very herbs from traveling salesmen.

To instill the Shuswap ethic in their young people, the elders told stories with morals. By night James Teit observed such moralizing in the tribes: The old people would address the young . . . and admonish them to follow the rules of proper ethical conduct (1909, 617). Such a practice was a prime example of how the Shuswap used a unique communication form, the Coyote stories, as an entertaining way to convey ethical instruction:

> *Storytelling was used to relay the many lessons of life. The mythical transformer, Coyote, was the central figure of these legends. Each Coyote story explained some aspect of nature or how some portion of the world had been created. Each adventure had a moral, instructing the Shuswap people how to live in harmony with nature and with one another. (Coffey et al. 1990, 39)*

The ethical fabric that children were taught included more than an underlying order of values—respect, sharing, stewardship, freedom, truthfulness, and responsibility. Shuswap ethics also included an invisible net of rules that proceeded from these values. As in all cultures the behavioral rules were particular. For example, during their menstrual cycle women were not to walk in front of men or touch any tools lest either became "contaminated" (Charlotte Christopher). Elders were "to be treated like royalty" (Rita Charlie), and "the dead were to be highly respected" (Antoine Archie).

Such rules pertained to so many areas of communication that a formidable list has been culled from interviews with elders and others. (This list below has the initials of the person interviewed in parentheses following each rule.) Shuswap communication rules from the "old days" included:

1. Be quiet when elders are speaking or enter (CC).
2. Make eye contact (DA).
3. Honor strange practices, superstitions, or ceremonies by participating in them to honor those who do (ID).
4. Avoid swearing or bad stories, particularly in the sweat lodge (ID).
5. Do not allow boys and girls of dating age to talk to each other privately (ID).
6. Do not gossip, particularly if it might hurt someone's reputation or family (CC, ID).
7. Always tell the truth (ID, CB).
8. If you break any of these rules in a serious and damaging way, you must be tried at a tribal court with the Chief presiding and pay a "fine" as punishment (DA, CB).
9. Do not laugh at other people (JA).
10. Do not laugh during religious ceremonies and funerals (JA).
11. After someone in your family dies, do not dance or celebrate for a year or more (ID).
12. Show proper manners and respect to all visitors (DA).
13. Do not interrupt other people's dialogue, particularly the elders or the chief (RC, EP).

14. Be careful and respectful with words (AD).

15. Pray for the people and nature; don't just pray for yourself (FJ).

16. Speak slowly; think before you speak (ER).

17. Welcome silence; speak only when you have something important to say (ER).

18. Be careful what you say about any living form; to criticize a person or animal is to blaspheme the gods since there is God in all life (FJ).

19. Interact with people's clothing and possessions as if with the person themselves; to sit on someone else's stool or wear his hat could hurt him or you (FJ).

20. Contain important information; do not tell outsiders, no matter how inquisitive they are, how to make sacred medicines, or perform special ceremonies (LH, ER, RC, AA).

21. Exercise extreme care in what you communicate to "the white man"; he may use it against you, sell it back to you, label it "heathen" and censor it; or steal it from you (RC, ER).

22. Do not complain openly of pain or admit suffering; be thick-skinned and tight-lipped (JJ, MAD).

23. Give tobacco as a gift to an elder before asking his or her advice (JJ).

24. Kneel before a chief, particularly if in a court (EP, FJ).

25. To respect other people's privacy, be silent when approaching or in their vicinity (MAD).

26. Respond to people so as to be accepting and nonjudgmental (MAD).

27. Show the humility that was built into the Shuswap language itself (e.g., language does not translate to "my house and your house," but rather approximately "my small house and your large house"; the language did not have swear words; etc.) (EP).

28. Do not complain or you are weak ("you were like a white

person if you complained . . . a weakness in your character")
(MAD, EP).

29. Do not depict symbols of death (the Owl, etc.) in your art
(NAD).

30. Keep some information even highly confidential from many
band members; elders or shamans serve as guardians for important secrets such as how to make special medicines, both
those for healing and those for poisoning (CC).

31. Unless spoken to, do not speak near authorities or people
with magic whom you fear (GE).

32. Show respect for arts ceremonies by participating or appro-
priately observing (LS).

33. Before any use of the Earth or its living forms, give a prayer
or a blessing; always connect with the Great Spirit at the outset of any important event (LS).

As these and many other invisible rules were learned, the
Shuswap child was trained in Shuswap "communication ethics"
without those foreign words and concepts ever being heard. Concepts such as "libel," "invasion of privacy," "freedom of speech,"
and other themes central to modern communication ethics
would have also sounded unduly abstract and alien to Native
sensibilities.

However, since such modern terms are now used throughout
the English-speaking world and on many reserves, it is useful to
consider what type of "communication ethics" early rules implied.
In terms of use modern ethical issues, the nineteenth-century
Shuswap

1. forbade slander and defamation of character (i.e., the damaging of reputation by gossip or accusation).

2. found sacrilege, blasphemy, or religious obscenity foreign to
their worldview.

3. thought sex to be healthy, free of later notions of guilt and shame introduced by European Christians so that sexual "obscenity" would have been alien to their thinking, although sexual education was private, discreet, and laconic.

4. classified information by degree of sacredness and power. Ceremonies of intimacy were not available to random outsiders and strong medicines or magic, particularly those that could heal or poison, were passed on by an inner elite to their trusted successors.

5. had ethical codes that were invisible and informal, yet strictly passed on by grandparents, parents, or aunts and uncles to children through example, discipline, instruction, and storytelling.

6. believed free speech was somewhat modified by age, gender, and position. Chiefs, elders, and other authorities had the most freedom of expression. They could be neither interrupted nor disturbed. Sweat ceremonies, "teenage" activities, and some rituals were segregated by gender.

7. thought invasion of privacy was more psychological than physical. Private "bedrooms" in lodges were rare, sexual intercourse was overheard by children, and there were few social secrets in the community. However, privacy was of a different order—to interrupt silence or natural sounds with the noise of endless chatter, collective babble, or machinery would have been considered highly intrusive or invasive.

8. did not formally censor the arts. However, traditional designs were more honored than radical experiments. Images of safety and health—of Eagle or Hawk—were preferred to undesirable images such as of Owl or a two-headed snake. While there were rules in the performing arts, spontaneity and change were welcome to some degree. However, such expression was primarily to bless and give thanks: dances, music,

or theater of a secular or destructive nature would have been indirectly censored through ostracism or deliberately banned.

9. found disturbing the peace unwelcome—laughter during sacred moments, outbreaks violating silence, and speaking when others "had the floor" were considered antisocial.

10. first saw mass media (the camera, the tape recorder, the radio, etc.) as unethical and ethical, depending on the "reserve" and the individual. Some elders feared the camera would steal their souls or the microphone would separate their voices from them, but most were amazed, amused, or enticed by new media. However, in several instances Natives were incensed by insensitive and intrusive use of the news media. Several ethical issues have been involved. Truthfulness, sensationalism, prejudicial coverage, intrusiveness, and copyright violation were among the most frequent.

11. found the communication of sexual and social equality unimportant. While both men and women have been chiefs and shamans, originally women were often excluded from important discussions and relegated to communicating with children and among themselves. Moreover, commoners had fewer communication rights than nobles, and slaves had virtually no rights.

Many, but not all, of these norms were common to other Indigenous People; however, some practices were unique to or more emphasized within the Salishan regions. The four greatest values —freedom, responsibility, truthfulness, and respect—underlying Shuswap ethics coincide with the values associated with many other Native tribes.

It would be an overgeneralization to say there was one Shuswap ethic. Values may well have differed slightly from band to band, and punishments for broken rules varied from chief to chief and council to council. Indeed, unlike the notion that all traditional societies were static, values also changed from generation to generation, often in subtle, imperceptible ways.

Moreover, rules of communication may also be easily oversimplified. For example, the rule "always tell the truth" in reality yielded to a double or even triple standard: tribe members might elect to speak truthfully to their families and friends but less openly to members of other bands who were allies for the moment, but with whom there had been tension six moons ago; a band member would deliberately lie to an enemy tribe, for example, if questioned about where his band resided. Telling the truth to the enemy might lead to the capture or massacre of his family.

Finally, while some Shuswap trusted some whites in some decades, frequently Natives followed the adage still quoted on some reserves: "First we learned to lie from the white man. Then we learned to lie to the white man." Once settlers had killed Indian game, sometimes in sport, most Shuswap were unlikely to tell settlers where the best hunting was, unless bribed with alcohol and other imported addictions.

In short, most communication rules were conditional. While one rule might state "always tell the truth," whether or not it was followed depended on who was speaking, to whom, on which topic, and with what degree of trust. Similarly, underlying values affirming the sacredness of all life did not guarantee that all Shuswap spoke respectfully or were equally sacred in their behavior.

## Modern Shuswap Views

Many Shuswap people understand the erosion of communion in their experience. Some elders blame rock and roll, MTV, and other media intrusions for disturbing the peace and encouraging an undisciplined lifestyle among their youth. Some advocate a return to their ancestral culture, while others wish to compete favorably with or within "the white man's world." Others search for a happy medium, or the best of both worlds. For many, the only viable option is whichever one will ensure survival.

Whichever path each individual takes, there are some specific communications many Shuswap people wish to make to the larger world. They find the notion that they are or were "primitive" or "savage" a sad misrepresentation in light of the elegance of their culture. "Primitive" and "savage" are also ironic terms since it was the European intruders and their diseases who eliminated most of the Shuswap and other Indigenous People.

Half-amused by the stereotype, modern Natives point out that many Native children who watch television wonder if *they* will encounter "Indians" in the forest or on a trip. It is shocking to discover that they are "Indians"—a misnomer possibly given by explorers who thought they had discovered India—in the eyes of others.

Fred Christopher of Canim Lake suggested that it is useful for people to visit the reserves and to travel from one to another, so that stereotypes are relinquished. Charlotte Christopher thinks such awareness, and other forms of education, generate "respect for one another's culture," which is reciprocally healthy. She feels it is important for non-Natives to also learn that there are "differences among Native groups and individuals just as there are among European countries and people."

Gary Emile emphasized the importance of more young people "learning to speak Shuswap." Embedded within the language itself are a multiplicity of subtle perspectives that tie Shuswap thoughts and humor more closely to the environment and their peers. Alkali Lake elder Laura Harry also underscored the Shuswap need for freedom. One of the most frequently voiced concerns that Shuswap elders (May Dixon, Ike Daniels, Laura Harry, and others) wished to communicate is that they had been fenced in by No Trespassing signs, property rights, roads, towns, and especially by ubiquitous fences. They feel at the least encaged and at the most enraged.

Many Shuswap people feel that they are viewed as isolated from Canadian culture. For example, Ike Daniels noted that few people realize how many Native people served in World War II and were decorated for bravery. In that war, one advantage of Shuswap communication was that Canadian Shuswaps could communicate in Shuswap without their messages being decoded by the Germans. "Many Shuswap volunteered . . . they weren't drafted," said Daniels, "and many were heroes." The opposite stance taken by some Natives from peaceful bands—to not fight "the white men's wars"—is no less noble. Both pacifism and heroic loyalty communicate signals contrary to media images of independent hostile warriors.

Perhaps the deepest concern of Shuswap people is racism. Images are put forth that they are lesser than, stupid, slow, heathen, inferior, obsolete, dirty, violent, drugged, and alcoholic. To the final two charges, they point out that such dependencies were introduced to Native societies by white traders. Alkali Lake, which in fourteen years changed from a 100 percent alcohol-dependent community to a 95 percent sober society, now provides a model of leadership for almost all Western societies, not just other Native communities. It is the stereotypes that are obsolete, not the Natives.

Like all other cultures, the Shuswap are replete with vices and virtues, children and parents, hearts and minds, humor and thought, arts and skills, pain and pride, universal tendencies and individual personalities. Each band and each person seeks to be seen as unique, yet bonded to a larger extended family. How their image and messages are presented to the world has as much to do with our communication and ethics as with theirs.

# CHAPTER SIX

*Navajo Medicine Man Leslie Francisco does a sandpainting for healing.*
*Photograph © by Marcia Keegan, 1994.*

# The Navajo People (Diné) of Arizona: A Case Study

It is jokingly said among some Diné that they now average five members in their families—two parents, two children, and a visiting anthropologist! Given the abundance of writing about the "Navajo" both by these anthropologists, and increasingly by their own historians, I will provide a much shorter summary of Diné history and culture than was provided about the seemingly more obscure Shuswap.

The focus of this chapter is on the *relationships* among (1) communication, (2) rules, and (3) ethics of the Diné, both in general and decades ago at the Rock Point, Arizona, reservation. Emphasis is given to the intersection of these three areas since they are minimally researched and almost universally misunderstood by outsiders. Moreover, this focus provides a parallel and comparison study to Shuswap communication. Finally, the *micro* studies of both groups (Shuswap and Diné) further ground and counterbalance the *macro* scope of the first three chapters.

## Who Are the Diné?

"Diné," meaning "the people," or "Dinée," meaning "tribe," "people," or "nation," is the original and preferred name of those people labeled "Navahu" by the Spanish. As stated within their own elaborate and beautiful creation story, the "Diné" originated from the first ("black") world. They then ascended through a "hole" into the second ("blue") world, then the third ("yellow") world, and into another (fourth) world in which they produced First Man and First Woman from two ears of corn. Following several other adventures in which the men abandoned the women, finally the two genders were reunited to climb into the fifth world (Zolbrod 1984, 1–78). A much fuller and more poetic rendering of the birth of the Diné people is found in *Diné Bahané: The Navajo Creation Story.*

Outsiders proffer a more pedestrian vision of "Navajo" origins. Citing the similarities of Natives in the United States and Asia, historians have suggested that the Navajo's ancestors migrated across the Bering Strait, perhaps as early as 30,000 B.C. (Jesse Jennings), or as late as 1,000 B.C. (James Spicer). Some believe the Navajo arrived in the Southwest as recently as A.D. 1400 (Spicer 1962, 283–290), or many centuries earlier (Kluckhohn and Leighton 1946, 33). But among the Diné there is also the notion that they descended from the Anasazi people, who may have lived at Chaco Canyon and Shiprock (New Mexico) as early as A.D. 1 (Rock Point Community School 1982, 70).

Some have tried to pinpoint the exact migration to time periods which show a slow migration of Asians across the Bering Strait (several centuries B.C.) down into the Pacific Northwest (first century A.D.), the mid-Pacific Coast (A.D. 400–700), and the Southwest (700–1,000 A.D.).

The history of atrocities perpetrated against the Diné are well documented. Landmark events include the widespread massacre of Diné sheep, causing starvation and debilitation in 1863, the "long walk" of 1864, the following confinement and desecration of eight thousand Navajo at Fort Sumner, the surrendering of their best land for the railroad, the endless violations of peace treaties, and, in general, their perpetual enslavement to imposed values and cultural genocide.

Despite this, the Navajo have been at various times the largest Native nation in the United States. They have usually possessed a territory greater than many independent nations.

My research, based on interviews at one reservation, represents far less than one percent of all the Diné tribes that have existed, many of which are extinct.

With walls made of earth and supported by timbers, the Diné's domed "hogans" housed extended families of parents, grandparents, many children, and sometimes aunts and uncles. Surrounding or near each hogan was the land of farmers, many of whom relied primarily on sheep-raising. Not only could sheep's wool be woven or traded, but mutton became a sustaining staple of the Diné diet.

Part of the Athabaskan linguistic family, the Diné lived throughout what are now called Arizona and New Mexico, amid neighbors such as the Zuni, Hopi, and Pueblo. Despite the decimation of large populations of Navajo in the last two centuries, there were at least 100,000 and possibly as many as 140,000 living on reservations by 1986.

The image of the Navajo as raiders, warriors, and nomads perpetuated by European settlers was in marked contrast to their own internal identity as holy people and farmers (Kluckhohn and Leighton 1946, 38). Their belligerence was more likely reprisal or self-defense. More important than war to the Diné was worship, since one-fourth of their waking time was spent in religious ceremony (Worth and Adair 1972, 39). Gary Witherspoon, who spent over fifteen years with the Diné, reports that more than sixty major rites and innumerable minor ones are still extant (1977, 13). Undoubtedly, the oldest and most sacred ritual is the

Blessing Way, which commemorates a meeting at which the Diné were taught to control the elements (Kluckhohn and Leighton 1946, 182). Devoted to many higher forms of expression, the Diné are an excellent nation from whom to learn about a large spectrum of communication.

## Diné Communication, Rules, and Ethics

While the Diné have become acclimated to modern mass media, they remain principally an oral society, using what Ralph Barney and John Maestas identify as the heart of tribal communication, "word of mouth" (1989, 1). Such reliance on spoken words is not mere preference, or laziness in utilizing technology. There is instead a profound trusting in the source and power of thought and language that outsiders are likely to miss or misinterpret.

For the traditional Diné thinking and singing have the power of creation and work together in balance. The counterpoint between the masculine "thinking" and the feminine "singing" (or sacred speaking) resonate with the underlying Diné values that Paul Zolbrod has discovered in their mythology: "Everything that happens . . . relates to the delicate balance of male and female" (1984, 6).

In Witherspoon's understanding, these two ritual components of creation, speech (including singing) and thought, have enormous powers. They may restore peace, harmonize a "patient" to his total environment, reenact creation, and change the very air from a negative to a positive spirit (1977, 17-25).

Air, the source of all life, may take the form of the "wind soul," or the animating interior force within each being. It is natural then, in a world of "air" or spirit, that the invisible world, where thought occurs, is essential and prerequisite to communication. In essence, positive thought will produce positive expression and action (Witherspoon 1977, 16).

From this philosophy is derived a unique communication ethic. Since language, like thought, may create or destroy all within the universe, one must be extremely careful in the choice of thoughts and words. After all, the word is the means by which all substance is not only created but also organized and transformed. Humor is essential to maintain lightness, since heaviness may cast too somber and sullen an atmosphere on the tribe.

The degree of discipline and control in employing words is revealed by the language itself—there are no superlatives or sensational adjectives, as if to avoid extremes in favor of the moderation central to Diné living. Nor can language be wasted. Often speech follows a lengthy silence, such that its partner, thought, will precede it.

Given this core philosophy, it is not surprising that Diné communication serves three primary purposes: blessing, curing, and purifying. (Witherspoon 1977, 13). Thought and song may *bless* any element in the Diné universe. There are rituals and words for blessing the land, livestock, crops, homes, property, relatives, and themselves. To harmonize the patient with his environment, there are specific communication *cures,* again through thought and song, for mental disorders, physical ailments, and environmental catastrophes. Finally, to communicate *purification* is, in essence, to verbally decontaminate any object after its inappropriate or inadvertent contact with dangerous spirits or objects (Witherspoon 1977, 13). An example of a blessing communication is the Hozhonji song entitled "Naestsan Biyin," or "Song of the Earth." On the left is the Diné lyric, as it appears in *The Indians' Book;* at the right is the English translation.

| NAESTSAN BIYIN | SONG OF THE EARTH |
|---|---|
| Daltso hozhoni, | All is beautiful, |
| Daltso hozho'ka', | All is beautiful, |
| Daltso hozhoni. | All is beautiful, indeed. |
| | |
| Naestsan-iye | Now the Mother Earth |
| Yatilyilch-iye | And the Father Sky, |
| Pilch ka' altsin sella | Meeting, joining one another, |
| Ho-ushte-hiye. | Helping ever, they. |
| | |
| Daltso hozhoni, | All is beautiful, |
| Daltson hozho'ka, | All is beautiful, |
| Daltso hozhoni. | All is beautiful, indeed. |
| | |
| Pilch da' altsin sella | Meeting, joining one another, |
| Ho-ushte-hiye. | Helpmates ever, they. |
| | |
| Daltso hozhoni, | All is beautiful, |
| Daltso hozho'ka', | All is beautiful, |
| Daltso hozhoni. | All is beautiful, indeed. |
| | |
| Ka' Doko-oslid-iye | Now Doko-oslid |
| Ka' Depensitsa-ye | And Depenitsa, |
| Pilch da'altsin sella | Meeting, joining one another, |
| Ho-ushte-hiye | Helpmates ever, they. |
| | |
| Daltso hozhoni, | All is beautiful, |
| Daltso hozho'ka' | All is beautiful, |
| Daltso hozhoni. | All is beautiful, indeed. |
| | |
| Ka' Tshalyilch, | And the night of darkness |
| Hayolkatli-ye, | And the dawn of light, |
| Pilch da' altsin sella | Meeting, joining one another, |
| Ho-ushte-hiye. | Helpmates ever, they. |

This song of beauty and balance continues for five more verses and choruses before concluding as it began:

| | |
|---|---|
| Daltso hozhoni, | Now all is beautiful |
| Daltso hozho'ka' | All is beautiful, |
| Daltso hozhoni. | All is beautiful, indeed. |
| | (Curtis, 1987, 372) |

Although nothing is said in the song about healing, purification, or blessing per se, one may sense its cathartic and inspirational value, in its reminding of the harmony and beauty of all. As one tribe member adds, "Our Hozhonji songs are like the Psalms of David. We sing them as a white man says his prayers. Our hero, Nayenezrani, is like the biblical hero David. By our Holy Ones were the songs made, even as the Bible was made by holy people" (cited in Curtis, 1987, 349). As Curtis further explains,

*This song . . . declares all things beautiful. It is highly revered and has great power to bless. It is a benediction on the created world. It tells how all things go in pairs, bending towards each other, joining and helping one another, as the heavens help the earth with rain. . . . Sometimes, after singing this Hozhonji-song, the Navajo sprinkles sacred pollen on the ground, calling the earth "Mother," and then scatters pollen upward to the sky, calling the heavens "Father." (1987, 371–376)*

Given this attitude of using communication to bless the surrounding world, one can see why the Diné questioned the introduction of the camera into their society. In *Through Navajo Eyes,* Worth and Adair noted Sam Yazzie's question, "Will making movies do the sheep any good?" when Yazzie was confronted with a camera. When he was told that it would not, he replied, "Then why make movies?" (1972, 4) If communication is not a blessing, he felt, of what purpose is it? Worth and Adair elaborate: "Their attitude toward photographing an animal or a house was similar to the attitude we have of 'borrowing' it." In borrowing an animal or house, we would entertain feelings of hesitancy, respect, and the urge to ask permission. "Why should it be different to photograph it, or tamper with its atmosphere in any other way?" the Diné wonder. If you "borrow," do you inherently bless, or do you impose? Most communication by white society has seemed more like imposition than blessing.

In this light, it is interesting to note that while Westerners closely associate communication with "freedom" (free speech, free press, etc.), the Diné associate it more closely with "responsibility" or "accountability." "If you lie, the gods will know," one elder told me, "so why lie?" As we discussed the matter further, she explained that one was responsible to the gods for what was said. Indeed in *An Analysis of Navajo Chantway Myths,* Katharine Spencer notes that Diné mythic heroes typically move from irresponsible to responsible action during the plot development (1957, 58–60). Responsibility and accountability are virtues to be modeled in living and in the arts.

Given this full-time responsibility, there is no separation between art and life. Both bear the responsibility of sustaining a divine rhythm and message. So art is not made to be enjoyed later, as in a gallery or recording. Rather the responsibility to be fulfilled and to be divine through art is known within the act of creation. In Witherspoon's words, "Beauty is not to be preserved but to be constantly renewed in one's self and expressed in one's daily life and activities. To contribute to and be a part of this universal ho' zho' is both man's special blessing and his ultimate destiny" (1977, 178).

Such a lifestyle has induced Dorothea Leighton to comment that "the White man practices his religion on Sunday; the Navajo observes his daily" (1947, 175). Although such stereotyping may be too simplistic, "around-the-clock" responsibility is accepted without question, doing "wrong" must be a conscious choice and a knowing avoidance of responsibility. Consequently, before doing wrong, a Native will *consciously* take the necessary measures that prevent ill effects, rather than casually sidestep responsibility (1947, 125).

Lying may be generally discouraged within a tribe, but there are many exceptions in the Diné communication ethic. For example, lying to preserve the welfare of the tribe and lying to strangers who may prove untrustworthy are condoned. One unique custom observed by Leighton is that, when confronted with an accusation that he is lying, a band member may remain silent the first three times but must tell the truth the fourth (1947, 131).

Such a rule reminds us that there are many *seemingly* peculiar communication rules among the Diné. Eye contact is usually avoided so as not to invade privacy. A mother-in-law and son-in-law are especially forbidden to look into each other's eyes (Kluckhohn and Leighton 1946, 201). The order of a ritual is absolute and never to be broken or reversed. Many subjects may only be discussed at various seasons or during certain parts of the day such as before or after sundown.

Despite the apparently arbitrary nature of these rules, most were developed for practical or spiritual reasons. Moreover, they would seem no more eccentric to an imaginary visiting, intelligent alien than many Western communication forms and rules. Imagine hearing or seeing yodeling, auctioneering, and cheerleading for the first time. Or imagine being taught communication rules such as mandatory genuflexion in front of a cross, curtsying before a Queen, or "flipping the bird" to a rival gang member. Is Diné communication any more strange? If a communication ethic were codified by the Diné, it would include many of the elements listed in chapter 3 in the Indigenous People's ethic (from *The Sacred Tree*). As noted by Kluckhohn and Leighton (1946, 291–313), Witherspoon, Spencer, Worth, Adair, and others, some prime ethical rules for Diné communicators would include the following:

1. Preserve and respect the ancient communication—do not embellish or distort teachings or chants.
2. Communicate with respect for the other individual—even a five-year-old's decision is worthy of consideration.
3. Communicate to the whole person, even to their psychosomatic illness or "evil spirits" and to their hidden feelings.
4. Communicate so as to cooperate with all of nature, which is more powerful than man. Discover the natural order and let the rules of communication follow the universal law.
5. Avoid excess. Minimal communication, free of ornate detail, and exclamation is to be valued.
6. Similarly, maintain even-tempered emotions. Avoid a display of temper and other disturbances of the peace.
7. Aim to help bring about consensus and unanimous decisions.
8. In general, communicate to all (except to the suspicious) as if they were your own relatives; be polite and open.
9. When in doubt, remain silent; let word and thought be sacred and substantial.

While a much longer code of ethics could be formulated, other guidelines would be primarily derived from these nine and from the central Diné philosophy described earlier. Research at Rock Point further expands this list and our overall understanding of Diné communication and ethics.

# Rock Point Communication, Rules, and Ethics

Those interviewed at the Rock Point Reservation in northeastern Arizona were asked about the old ways of communicating prior to outside encroachment. All were asked about their earliest memories and the most ancient stories and memories told them by their elders and the elders' elders. Although there are no surviving Diné totally uninfluenced by America's government and immigrants, I endeavored to find those least encumbered by American culture as well as those most encumbered, that is, those fully educated in the U.S. system who could thus compare the two cultures and mindsets. Within the latter category, I also interviewed two white educators, Dan McLaughlin and Clyde Duncan, who had lived with the Diné at length and, in Clyde's case, married into the Diné community, such that they had a unique basis for empathy and comparison.

The Diné interviewed ranged from such senior respected leaders as Thomas Littleben, age 70, to such junior leaders as Princeton-educated Rex Lee Jim, age 26. More elder than younger people and more permanent than cosmopolitan (traveled) residents were chosen. Slightly fewer women than men were interviewed, although equal numbers would have been preferred.

Some of those interviewed preferred to be anonymous (referred to below as "an educator," or a "shepherd," etc.), and most opted to have their English name listed. Out of deep respect for my Rock Point associates, I have honored all requests for confidentiality, anonymity, privacy, deferred questions, and the limits to sacred areas of discussion.

Although this section is about communication, rules, and ethics, it should be remembered that some of the myths and memories extend to a time before the Rock Point Reservation existed. Moreover, all those living at Rock Point did not originate there. Some interviews revealed that those living on reservations may have moved from or married someone from another reservation. Finally, those living at Rock Point, like many modern Indigenous People, had been socialized to varying degrees by outside influences: some watched television; some listened to radio; some read magazines and newspapers; some had many or a few Anglo or Hispanic friends; only a few tried to totally preserve traditional values.

With all these qualifications in mind, one may still discern common patterns in the "old" Rock Point Diné communication ethic.

## SPECIFIC CULTURAL RULES

Traditionally, eye contact had several rules. It was avoided or utilized according to the subject discussed. Since eye contact was almost always avoided with strangers to avoid intimacy, settlers received the false impression that all Diné always avoided eye contact. When entering a hogan, it was necessary to walk clockwise around the periphery before sitting down. When speaking, not only was one silent first, but often one gestured prior to speaking.

Due to their wealth, medicine men could have more than one wife, and there was a pecking order for communication with and among the wives.

## SACRED VERSUS PRACTICAL RULES

Often more than a dozen people lived in one hogan, so many communication rules were practical, such as those establishing who could speak first so everyone did not speak at once. Usually, more senior people and members of one's clan (extended family) were given the most respect when speaking. But there were also deeper, more sacred rules that were intuitively discerned. As Diné educator Bobby Begay and Diné linguist/translator Thomas Benally articulated, there were "modes" of communicating, such as "inner" versus "outer."

To communicate from the inside meant to maintain awareness that there were "holy beings" everywhere, that all senses were sacred, and that each being and object had a gender (male or female) to be respected and addressed. During sacred moments, this larger inner awareness would be foremost in consciousness, so as to communicate with far greater inner respect than when casually joking outwardly or teasing a friend.

## MORAL RULES

Diné customs carried a strong sense of what the West would call morality. Boys could only learn about sex by discussing it with a father or paternal uncles, while girls frequently learned from their aunts. Subjects such as incest and other taboos were particularly to be avoided. To discuss death, particularly of family members, was considered immoral. Any form of arrogance, or seeming arrogance, was to be shunned. Mocking of the holy world, whether in conversation or satirical imitation, was unthinkable.

## SLANDER, BLASPHEMY, AND OTHER DEFAMATION

Respectful thoughts and words were essential to Diné. For example, given the power of thoughts and words to create forms, one should never discuss lightning, thunder, or tornados during rain. Similarly, speaking negatively of other people was twice cursed—it could damn or disturb those talked about, but similarly, because it was negative, and because "negative is rewarded with negative," bad words might boomerang and hurt the speaker. Speaking badly of plants and animals is no less dangerous, given their supernatural powers. Blasphemy was a meaningless concept, since to even think of demeaning the Gods would result in harsh Divine retribution. Similarly, obscenity had little meaning since originally sex was healthy, and family training was so firm, one would not engage in "deviant" alternatives such as necrophilia or bestiality.

Respectful language meant to avoid words with even possible negative connotations such as "ghost" or "crazy." While there was no law specifying types of slander, virtually all forms of naysaying were punished with some form of peer disapproval, from minor judgment to full-scale ostracism. Since reputation and personal honor were central to Diné identity, gossip and accusations were hard to live down and thus were strongly discouraged. As Thomas Littleben noted, cursing was also forbidden within the hogan, since the hogan itself was sacred (interview 8/20/90).

## CENSORSHIP AND THE ARTS

Within Diné art it was traditional to represent nature, divinity, and symbols. Thus questions of how much nudity or intercourse to depict did not arise. However, the arts were not so much censored as prescribed. The emphasis was on which images should be depicted rather than on which were prohibited.

For example, in a sand painting that a healer used in a curing ceremony, only specific images would be effective in healing, so other images would have no purpose. Similarly, only certain people might contribute to the ceremony. Children were excluded from seeing the creation of sand paintings, not because of censorship but because their presence might crowd or disrupt the ceremony. In effect those with acquisitive or violating attitudes

were also censored. Paul Jones, the Rock Point trading post man-
ager for eighteen years, remembered that once an outsider had
offered $250 to see a ceremony. The aggressive curiosity seeker was
refused on the basis of his attitude, one in sharp contrast with the
nature of the ceremony.

## INVASION OF PRIVACY

On the one hand, "privacy" was a foreign notion, since there was
a widespread information grapevine about local incidents. On the
other hand, one's "soul" and thoughts were private, and those who
inquired about or intruded into such personal matters were not
to be trusted.

Indeed, to take what did not belong to one's self, such as by
taping sacred songs, ceremonies, and prayers, was both theft and
invasion. When prayers and ceremonies were taped and trans-
ported to other locations, they were removed from a *private*
ceremonial location into a public and foreign one. As Bobby
Begay indicated, electricity, like lightning, was to be feared more
than welcomed. So machines like the tape recorder, which relied
on electricity and which seemed to disembody the spirit, approached a type of witchcraft that entered the private envelope of
identity and "trapped" one's essence with lightning. This type of
"internal rape" was much more psychologically intense to the
Diné than the usual outsider's notion of "invasion of privacy."

## TRUTH-TELLING

Both a shepherd and an elder stressed that "lying" was the "white
man's" form of communication. "In the old days," Thomas Littleben reported, "your mother would whip you each time you lied,
so you learned not to." One was disgraced to choose words

unwisely, and thus especially disgraced to chose inaccurate or deceptive words. If you lied, it was inferred or even spoken that you had "stooped" to the coarser levels of expression imported by Spaniards and cowboys.

Decades ago, the chief of a tribe delivered "the word of truth" from a horse, so as to rise above others and let an absolute mandate ring forth. His word was originally considered an ultimate truth or command. Similarly the "medicine men," or doctors, would have candid talks while seated in a ring and impart the true and exact words for ceremonies. In these senses "truth" meant more than accuracy or the absence of deception. In the sense that many religions or philosophies speak of an "ultimate Truth," the Diné sensed an exact power that, when converted to thought and speech, became, in Western terms, Truth.

## MORAL INSTRUCTION

Given the avuncular kinship structure of Diné families, much moral training came from uncles, rather than parents or churches. Similarly, given the balance sought between men and women, usually the eldest woman determined and expressed the ethical norms for the extended family. First the child was taught how to listen. Later she or he was told the stories that presented moral instruction. Socialization had many forms—peer influence, punishment, role models, and special ceremonies, such as the puberty rite of passage, which also instructed one about how to be mature. Teaching was constantly enforced by the overall value system expressed through family and tribal living.

## RULES ABOUT SPEAKING

Given the clan family arrangement, one was more likely to speak to family members than others. Until one was seventeen or eighteen it was polite to be "seen and not heard" as a child, to respect and not interrupt the words of elders. Interclan rules were exacting: one could tease a mother about the clan she married into, but not tease a grandmother.

Rules governing silence before speaking were manifold. Innumerable ceremonies, such as a stargazing or healing ceremony, called for purposeful silence, such as to sense what was causing the ill health of the patient. It was considered rude to immediately seize the floor after another had finished speaking, rather than granting a silent moment for the preceding speech to sink in. Often the doctor would call for a period of silence, just as nature would ask for silence by bringing rain, thunder, wind, or other meaningful communiqués.

When tempted to laugh at someone, it was best to remain silent. Laughing at anyone was taboo, but laughing at elders, leaders, and the physically impaired was especially to be avoided.

Laughing *with* rather than *at* was strongly encouraged, although strangers often remained too distant to observe the humor. Hence there was a frequent misinterpretation of the silent, serious faces as straight-laced sobriety.

## CEREMONY

Great singers and dancers built reputations after many years of hard work. Their respect from the community depended on their degree of discipline and effectiveness in their work, such as casting out spirits or ceremonially protecting the sheep. Hence there was an intensive commitment to rehearsal prior to performance. Inherent to sacred ceremony were the rules "practice makes alignment" and "be aligned with the divine before you perform." As Genevieve Begay pointed out, those being healed or inducted also often had a specific responsibility—to rise early and prepare, to listen intently, to summon a spirit one's self, to follow ordered instructions, or just to remain humble.

Ceremonies were not limited to therapy or art. They provided a direct covenant with the "powers that be." Just as the absence of chant in some monasteries has been linked with a disintegrating morale, so some Diné link the erosion of Native ceremony with the hardships of the community. Ceremony created outer protection and inner strength. So the disappearance of ceremony consequently led to intrusion and weakness. So think many of the elders.

## OVERVIEW

Thomas Littleben notes that the Diné "cannot exist without prayer—it's our very life." Prayerful singing, dancing, thinking, and speaking constitute the practice of a communicated ethic. Other rules and expressions extend from this inner core.

The cynical explorers who first met the "Navajo" held that such zealousness allowed the "red men" to ensure themselves against misfortune by currying favor with the gods. A more innocent interpretation suggests that the Diné are simply a deeply spiritual and thankful people who pray by nature. By virtue of their constant association with the natural world they feel and see constant reminders of the myth and mystery conveyed through their ancestors.

A particular humility is necessary before assuming that one understands the Diné people. Since "containment" is a primary tenet of their communication ethic, no researcher may ever be sure how much of the Diné world has been "contained" and thus remains secret to outsiders, no matter how trusted.

*Navajo weaver Mae Chee Castillo in front of her hogan on the Navajo Reservation. Mae Chee herds her sheep near her home. Photograph © by Marcia Keegan, 1976.*

One of the recurring forms of "deception" that was traditionally practiced among the Diné was the "denial" by the medicine man. When asked a particular healing secret or sacred saying, he would deny that he knew the answer or he refused to speak. Those being "denied" felt that such doctors contained more wisdom than they revealed.

Similarly, one can never know all that the Diné internally communicated. However, from what is known, one can be sure of the communication ethic that would have surrounded the protected inner order—an ethic of respect, balance, containment, moderation, and especially reverence.

# CHAPTER SEVEN

*Images engraved on wooden song boards served as memory aides for chants sung during the Midewiwin ceremonies of the Ojibway. Here a fish and beaver seem to be talking. Drawing © by Sabra Moore.*

# A Singular Ethic: Spirituality and Source

*The supreme law of the land
is the Great Spirit's, not man's law.*

Thomas Banyacya, Sr.
(quoted in *Arden and Wall* 1991, 95)

In the quotation above, the famed interpreter of Hopi prophecies, Thomas Banyacya, Sr. affirms that the primary source of Native behavior is spiritual. What outsiders call "ethics" are derivative from a *singular* ethic, inseparable from the Great Spirit's law. Throughout the Indigenous world the "Great Spirit," a translation probably coined by Western interpreters, was known by other names—Wakantonka, the Old One, First Man and First Woman, Eagle, Ku, Kora, the Gods, Windwalker, Sun, Monka, Coyote, and others—but this spirit is always the source of all, including "communication" and "ethics."

The primary communication of Native People was not with each other but with the Great Spirit. As Chief Leon Shenandoah, of the Six Nations Iroquois Confederacy, stated, "Our religion is all about thanking the Creator. That's what we do when we pray. We don't ask Him for things. We thank him. We thank him for everything that exists" (Arden and Wall 1991, 105).

Such thankfulness produced an atmosphere surrounding Natives which was distinctly different from that surrounding European conquerors with a demanding or demeaning expression. To the extent that a person perceived with his heart a deep level of communication with Nature, rather than merely conceived in her head that such was going on, communion occurred.

## Communion and Communication

It is said that Thoreau and landscape artists "communed" with nature. Such people seem to have in common that they opened their internal radar and sonar to the subtle country sounds, sights, and smells that are drowned out by city living. This notion of "communion" somewhat approached the Native "precontact state," but was *relatively* superficial and preliminary. Most Indigenous People never needed to go elsewhere to hear, smell, sense, or see a wide zoological, botanical, and paranormal spectrum. It was their common abode and that of innumerable generations of ancestors. Relative to immigrant cultures, they were long-standing connoisseurs of the elements; talking to healing herbs was as natural as talking to each other.

Consequently, animals, plants, spirits, weather patterns, and humans were all part of one comingled society. Communion— a common sensing of the seasonal, spiritual, and ecological rhythms—was an unspoken language known by all. At its core was the bedrock sense that all life was sacred. Whatever differences separated plants from animals, or humans from the wind, all were holy and could perceive each other's sacred essence. In this sense, communication pertained more to silent discernment, inner listening, intimate sensing, subtle observation, and uncommon perception, not the raw imparting of information or emotion.

Eisley, Muir, Audubon, and other naturalists have indicated what is possible when living with or near other species: hidden animal activities become familiar, bird greetings may be answered, humans may become somewhat welcomed into protected worlds. As amazing as this coexistence seems, it is shallow relative to a state in which tribal members serenaded the trees and saw them bend to reply. Imagine foxes and wolves waiting each morning for their Native friends to arise and travel together for water and common game in the valley. Communion was not a state to be attained but was the organic unmediated interaction *already* present.

It was not easy for the educated Westerner to understand this notion with his intellect. As Seminole Medicine Man Buffalo Jim implored urban interviewers, "Ask me questions from your heart and I'll give you answers from my heart" (Arden and Wall 1991, 78). Such a sentiment was echoed by an anthropologist from the Easter Islands, Sergio Rapu: "You cannot understand Polynesia with your head; you must understand and feel Polynesia with your heart" (interview 1990). In the Polynesian view, "all things are spiritual and all things are part of a consciousness that never ends" (interview, Rapu 1990).

Buffalo Jim and Sergio Rapu imply that spiritual language is not understood by a sophisticated analysis of its syntax but by tuning in to the tone behind the words. If the speaker expresses with a closed heart, from a mental posture, then spirit cannot be expressed. The listener will back away or continue with suspicion. Only in the open-hearted mode is the speaker deemed genuine and thus to be trusted. Such open-hearted speaking is evidence of verbal communion, just as inner listening is evidence of silent communion.

Ultimately, it is the tone—*tone* of voice, tone of character, tone of atmospheric milieu, tone of thought—that is the important carrier wave for Native People. Just as it is said that an animal can sense fear in human beings, or that a great detective has a "sixth sense" for criminal clues, Native People can sense otherwise sacred messages in the tone behind the sound, the atmosphere surrounding the event, the attitude of a stranger, and the timbre of a chant.

A Kiowa tale, narrated by N. Scott Momaday, dramatically illustrates the importance of tone:

> *When I was a child, my father told me the story of the arrow maker; and he told it to me many times for I fell in love with it. I have no memory that is older than that of hearing it. This is the way it goes: If an arrow is well-made, it will have tooth marks on it. The Kiowas made fine arrows and straightened them in their teeth. Then they drew them to see that they were straight.*
>
> *Once there was a man and his wife. They were alone at night in the tepee. By the light of a fire, the man was making arrows. After a while, he caught sight of something. There was a small opening in the tepee where two hides had been sewn together Someone was there on the outside looking in. The man went on with his work but he said to his wife, "Someone is standing outside, do not be afraid. Let us talk easily as of ordinary things." He took up an arrow and straightened it in his teeth. Then, as it was right for him to do, he drew it to the bow and took aim; first in this direction and then in that.*
>
> *And all the while he was talking as if to his wife, but this is how he spoke. "I know that you are there on the outside, for I can feel your eyes on me. If you are a Kiowa, you will understand what I am saying and you will speak your name." But there was no answer, and the man went on in the same way, pointing the arrow all around. At last, his aim fell on the place where his enemy stood and he let go of the string. The arrow went straight to the enemy's heart. (1976, 303)*

One becomes aware of the heightened sensory world of the Kiowa when the arrow maker says, "I can feel your eyes on me." But it is the sustained tone of voice that is essential to the survival of the arrow maker and his wife, and it is the sustained tone of voice that provides the clever turning point in the plot.

In this sense, the key dialogue in the text is when the arrow maker says to his wife, "Let us talk easily of ordinary things." Because they "talk *easily*," because there is no change in tone, the stranger is not alarmed. Because his assurance cannot be clouded by fear, the arrow maker's voice remains unbroken, his tone remains even, his spirit seems normal. This is the mode of communication to which his hidden adversary responds, with the *spirit* of the arrow maker's voice.

It is this undisturbed vocal rhythm and tone that allow the arrow to find the heart of its target. This realization is the perfect metaphor for Native communication—if there is the unbroken, unwavering, assurance of communion (in this case not only with Spirit but with his wife), then whatever communication proceeds from that tone will find the heart of its audience. If, however, the communion (the assured connection with the divine) is disturbed, the arrow of communication will fly off target, like a golfer who has lost concentration or a karate champion who has broken confidence.

Earlier Momaday has noted what the steadfast central tone is like for the Native communicator: "The singer stands at the *center* of sound, of motion, of life. Nothing within the whole sphere of being is inaccessible to him or lost on him. . . . He knows something about himself and about the world in which he lives and he knows that he knows. He is essentially at peace" (1976, 294). It is from this state of perceived oneness that accurate communication exudes.

Similarly, if fear, judgment of the gods, disrespect, or some similar attitude has violated the singer's alignment, the arrow will miss its mark, and miscommunication will betray spiritual impotency. No wonder the psychic battles between rival "medicine men" and "witch doctors" were often translated as a "battle of wills" by Westerners. What was really happening was an engagement between spiritual forces until the assurance of one party melted in the presence of a "greater voltage" and higher authority.

A similar mistranslation informed the way European and American soldiers assessed Native warriors. Indigenous Peoples often received the English appellation "braves" as an abbreviation for their assumed bravery in battle. Yet the notion of bravery suggests a daring stance that had to be attained by risk-taking and ambition. In fact, the spiritual warrior felt that if communion with the gods were exact, it was only natural that his arrows would be guided, his body would be protected, or, if he died, his valor would be rewarded. In this sense bravery was not so much what was needed as an absolute trust in the guardian spirits of the battle. If the training was fully disciplined and the trust was consistent, the arrow would find the heart of its target.

Living in communion meant unveiling the essential reality of what was already present. It is no surprise, then, that accounts flourish which describe Natives talking to the earth, or listening for the earth's heartbeat, to discover the world's rhythm and wishes. In many tribes, such as the Shuswap and Carrier, the ceremonial drum was called "the heartbeat," as if the pulse of the earth, or of life, could be translated into humanly produced sound. After all, the essence of communion was to be in synch with the forces of life—music was for amplifying the rhythms already in evidence, not for producing artificial or unusual sounds, no matter how attractive or seductive.

At the heart of this pulsing expression was *naturalness*. From the moment a baby was in the womb, listening to the mother's

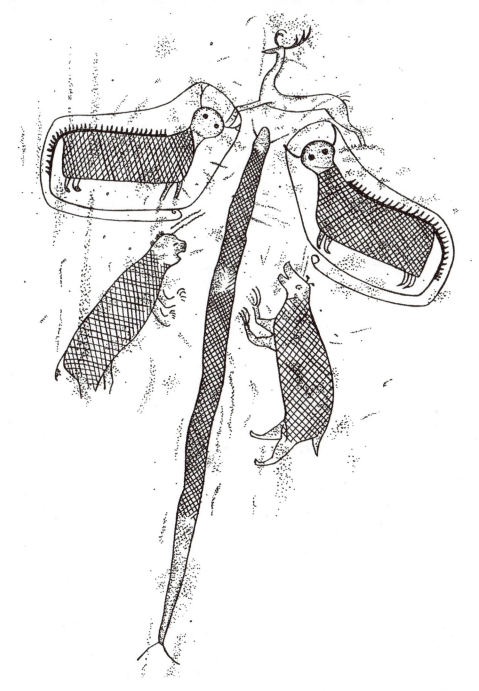

*Detail from drawings incised on a Winnebago antler club, showing mythological beings, possibly underwater panthers (encircled) flanking a snake and other creatures. Native artists often engraved images of spirit helpers onto weapons. Drawing © by Sabra Moore.*

heartbeat, symmetrical rhythms were at the center of her perceived world. It is not surprising, then, that percussion is and was
a universal expression of Indigenous People. The consistency of
rhythms expressing the Great Spirit—the lapping of the waves, the
whispering of the wind, the changing of the seasons, the thunder-
ing of the sky, the heartbeat of all Beings (even the rocks and
plants were assumed to have life energy)—reminded tribal people
that all life was rhythmic, connected, and divine.

In essence, communion was simply attunement, alignment,
"at oneness" with life's itinerary. To cut down a tree was a violation of this natural force. To let trees grow was to honor the
natural forces already in effect. Cutting even a branch, required
special permission of the tree. To speak without purpose, to make
up a nonsense song, or to glibly reply to a question, was to be
artificial, to violate natural attunement, to cut a consciousness tree
without reason or permission.

Ultimately, spirituality and living were synonymous. The
Western pioneer thought the Native lived a fragmented life con-
sisting of unrelated rituals, meals, fights, hunts, and work. Yet
there was a unified tempo connecting all these activities that the
insider perceived and sought to preserve. What the gods had
bequeathed to humans were the processes of living—sleeping,
chewing, swallowing, walking, seeing, listening, excreting, stoop-
ing, running, copulating, drinking, breathing. If these processes
were honored without artifice or abuse, humans would creatively
use their bodies in the ways designed by the gods.

Similarly, if the tongues, hands, and lips could be used simply
to make natural human sounds and images, to blend with the
natural world, an expression of communion could not only be felt
but articulated as well. While the white man lumped these
expressions into the modern concept of "communication,"
"ritual," or "art," the Native could not separate them from "the

way things work," from organic processes, natural law, attunement, communion.

While many missionaries emphasized the Native's worship of "pagan idols" and totems, these outsiders were usually oblivious to the deeper spiritual processes at work. It was not the *religious* bowing to *external* phenomena that *most* characterized Native worship, but the *internal* spiritual climate that determined the presence of communion. Without such spiritual expression, there could be no meaningful communion. And without genuine communion, there could be no meaningful communication. Thus the entire communication ethic was firmly based on spiritual communion.

## The Word, Words, Chant, and Power

In previous chapters, many diverse functions of Native words have been mentioned: words offer blessings, curses, magic, divine connection, reconnection, practical information, naming, mystery, and feelings. In this section, a deeper discussion of *how* words, sounds, and language evoke spirit, spirits, and spiritual power is presented.

At the outset it should be noted that every culture has ways of linking or equating human sounds with the divine. A central tenet of Christian theology is quoted from the beginning of the New Testament Gospel of John, "In the beginning was the word, and the word was with God, and the word was God" (John 1:1). In Western civilization, a gifted vocalist "sings like an angel." A great composer's notes "fall straight from Heaven," as was said about Mozart by his peers. To some, Handel's "Hallelujah Chorus" connected mortal man to the gods and made of man either "a King of Kings and Lord of Lords" or "the one who worshiped the King of Kings and Lord of Lords through song."

*Twin figure petroglyphs from the Columbia River area, their heads emanating "halos" of spiritual power. These beings probably appeared to the vision seeker shown as a small figure in the center. At puberty, children would visit these remote petroglyph sites to seek a spirit helper, then add their pecked marks or images. Drawing © by Sabra Moore.*

It should not be surprising, then, to note that many Native tribes view musical chant as an activity in which spirit operates freely through man. The open vowels at the end of most chanted words let sounds sustain and ascend, as if to higher dimensions. Some chants use "nether words," sounds that are neither word nor nonsense sound, but rest between those two forms, as if to imply wordlike meanings, but transcend concrete definition. Such sounds could be called "spirit sounds" in that they invite the listener and chanter to enter an altered state without being distracted by detailed content.

Other chants repeat a few words, such as "Daltso Hozhoni," a phrase evoking deep happiness. Often dozens of repetitions are required, until one or more of these three conditions have been attained: (1) the singer fully contemplates and experiences the meaning of the words, (2) he is no longer distracted by the environment, or (3) she ascends to higher levels of bliss and awareness.

Sometimes completely open vowels are chanted in primal societies. The meaning of the music comes from the experience of the pure sound, as in playing a note on an instrument, not from conscious interpretation of the sound's meaning, as when lyrics are employed. Such sounds seem "of the gods," in that the human voice is used in its most pure, untutored mode without man-made vocal constructions (words) imposed on any utterance.

In many societies chanting is the form closest to breathing, each being rhythmic, oral, pure, innocent, often unconscious processes. In many societies breathing is a sacred activity and some groups teach a disciplined form of breathing to their children. Among the early Shuswap a shaman's breathing and blowing on the sick might allow their health to return. Since breath, like the wind, is a symbol of the invisible movement of Spirit(s), and is also the rhythmic source of life, breathing is often a revered contact point with the spirit world.

To the European settlers and explorers the world of breathing, speaking, and singing was second nature, and thus often subconscious or transparent. However, such processes were not to be taken for granted by Aboriginals. Consider these excerpts from Joachim Berendt's *Nada Brahma: The World Is Sound* (1987) and their insights about the perceived relationships among our primary oral activities:

> *When we study the science of breath the first thing we notice is that breath is audible; it is a word in itself, for what we call a word is only a more pronounced utterance of breath fashioned by the mouth and tongue. In the capacity of the mouth breath becomes voice, and therefore the original condition of a word is breath. If we said "First was the breath," it would be the same as saying "In the beginning was the word." (33)*

> *Confucius considered that while words contain genuine meanings which reflect certain absolute truths in the universe, most people have lost contact with these truths and so use language to suit their own convenience. This led, he felt, to lax thinking, erroneous judgments, confused actions and finally to the wrong people acquiring access to political power. (41)*

> *The Latin word* cantare *is generally translated as "to sing." Its original meaning, however, was "to work magic, to produce by magic." One can sense the transition that must have taken place somewhere in time: in the process of working magic through primal sounds, evoking metamorphoses through sounds, man musicalized these sounds—he sang. (47)*

> *The words for "poet," "singer," and "magician" go back to the same linguistic root not only in Latin but in many other languages. Quite often they all have the same meaning, which makes sense when one considers the magician's main tool, language—or more precisely: the word. (55)*

For both the author and for many Indigenous People, breathing, speaking, chanting, and singing are activities to be consciously respected, contemplated, and connected to a larger web of meaning.

Such thinking illuminates many assumptions of the Native's word world—the symbiosis between music and magic, the common origin of speaking and praying, the parallel pulse of breathing and speaking, and the spirit(s) released through these outlets for sound. If they were voiced in other cultures, they would strongly resonate within the Aboriginal ambience.

Linguistics scholars and psychologists locked in the debate over whether thought creates language or whether language creates thought might consider the Native alternative—"spirit creates both." Consider Rubellite Johnson's discussion of the Hawaiian Kinolau. She lists over two dozen words beginning with the prefix *Ku* and over four dozen beginning with the prefix *Kane*. Both Ku and Kane were gods whose presence could be felt in numerous natural phenomena. For example, "Ku-mauna" meant "God of the mountain," while "Ku-ka-o'o" meant "Ku of the digging stick." "Kane-i-ke-anuenue" translates "Kane in the rainbow," while "Kane-i-ka-puahiohio" means "Kane in the whirlwind" (1991, 1, 2, 5–8).

Thus the language (and the thought) echoed what was innately first perceived, then later conceptualized: if a Polynesian god named Pulua seemed present in an earthquake, then future earthquakes might be called Pulua-eo-inake, or "God acting through the shaking earth." Similarly, the naming of people could relate to their true spiritual identity. For example, a holy or saintly person might be called Noble Elk in a tribe that venerated Elk's divinity.

It is by no means astonishing that this naming process imbued many words with power. To say a word beginning with Ku or Kane was to invoke the spirit of Ku or Kane. Some sentences spoken by chiefs and doctors (not "witch doctors," a condescending misnomer) seemed like a scientist passing a Geiger counter over many samples of uranium. As the sacred words were pronounced, their radioactive charge was felt by all in the vocal intonation, if not the entranced posture, of the speaker.

Indeed, some words were only to be spoken by those who preserved a society's spiritual integrity. For example, Philip Peek encountered "hidden" words during his research in Africa:

> During my ethnohistorical fieldwork among the Isoko, elders would frequently use eme didi ("hidden words" or "deep" Isoko), archaic speech which only elders can use. If my interpreters did anything more than "mechanically" translate, if they used those words or interpreted their meaning, the elders immediately stopped talking and waited for the young man (usually in his late thirties) to apologize for his transgression. While many people may understand some eme didi, none but the elders may use them or indicate comprehension of their real meaning. (1981, 36)

Just like the "soft words" and "containment" mentioned in previous chapters, *eme didi* indicates a level of sacredness to be kept in the "inner court," or, in the English vernacular, signifies pearls that are not to be cast before swine. Throughout the history of religions, it is common to find that "the best" was to be saved for the gods. While it is frequently noted that "the best" of the harvest was to be fed to the gods, or the finest (animal) or purest (virgin) was to be sacrificed to the gods, it is seldom considered that the words of finest sound and meaning were also preserved for rare and rarified use, such as when contacting the gods. Thus it is not unusual that such words were often "protected" within a caste of those deemed the most mature, senior, and righteous.

Those using divine language often also *needed* protection. In describing the "channeling" of the Nigerian Yoruba storyteller, Peek noted this danger:

> Words can affect their speaker, and the speaker must take precautions to guard himself from the adverse effects of the words' power. Numerous examples of this identification of the verbal artist and his words are provided by southern Nigerian people. In the very appropriate description of the Yoruba storyteller as a "medium, "LaPin stresses that the narrator "not only tells the story, but in a very real sense he becomes it." This description is not intended in the familiar sense of the storyteller merely acting out a tale; rather for the Yoruba, a storyteller is a medium who is literally possessed by a tale (which is considered a 'reincarnation'). (1981, 37)

Thus, one danger is due to surrendering to an altered state in which ancestors, spirits, and other disembodied powers seek an "open" body to use as their conduit for messages. Training and precautions are essential to enact this process without psychological and sometimes physical repercussions.

For the "medium," communication is divine in the most direct sense. Mediums convey messages *while* they are being transmitted. Other communicators may relay *indirect* divine messages. For example, in some tribes although a song *once* came from the gods, it has been handed down from father to son, or from master singer to disciple, in the interim. Here are some examples of divine inspiration that came *before* rather than *during* the ceremony:

> Biebuyck notes that among the Lega and Mongo peoples of Central Africa, bards who perform heroic epics are thought to have received their knowledge from ancestors or powerful nature spirits. If a priests of the Yoruba assert that spirit

> *messengers come at night to teach them new verses to use during divination sessions. Babalola reports as well that Yoruba Ijala chanters receive divine inspiration from the orisa (deity) Ogun. Herskovits learned in Dahomey (now Benin) that some songs "come into the heads" of initiates of certain cults and "are interpreted as the voice of the deity himself."* (Peek 1981, 30)

Thus a variety of means for divine communication present themselves. One may speak like a God, to a God, indirectly for a God, as a God's conduit or megaphone, as a God's delayed messenger, after the tutelage or mentorship of a God, after dreaming of a God, and any other number of ways of contacting, conveying, or representing Gods and Goddesses.

However, all these means are secondary to the most powerful voicing among the Indigenous—speaking *as* a God or Goddess. The very act of verbal expression is often considered divine, so to speak is to be godlike. The sounds that proceed from within a person are often interpreted as a spirit coming forth. Just as in some societies, the blood that flows from a cut is viewed as an escaping spirit, even so escaping words or notes from within characterize one's divine identity. As Placied Tempels describes in *Bantu Philosophy*, "A living man's words or his gesture are considered, more than any other manifestation, to be the formal expression or sign of his vital influence" (1969, 54).

Just as in Western societies an individual is *finger*printed to delineate unique identity, in Indigenous societies, it is often the *voice*-print that identifies the inner and thus real person. In describing the Dinka of the Sudan, Deng writes "honor, dignity, and inner pride as well as their outward appearance and bearing are part of what the dinka call *dheeng*, which has many meanings. Singing, as an expression of one's personality, is *dheeng*" (1993, 16).

The voice, because it conveys one's inner world and carries the envelope of surrounding emotions, may frequently be seen as the birthmark of one's spiritual identity. In adversarial experiences, the voice becomes the tube through which one blows verbal darts to the heart of an opponent. Yet in ceremonial moments, the voice is a specialized instrument that uniquely blends divinity with identity. If the eyes are the "place where the light shines out," the mouth is the orifice where the "soul leaks out" or the "spirit pours forth."

It is not surprising that Westerners eventually categorized Native Peoples as *oral* societies. To most tribes the mouth was sacred, the tongue was God-given, and to the Maori, even the upper and lower jaw had specialized functions. Thus the "forked tongue" was not simply destructive due to its deception. A cleft tongue also blocked and divided the free flow of spirit and the pure release of the soul. Forked tongue substituted *inferior* identity for the expression of *interior* identity.

## Ultimate Communication

In a modern electronic society, "ultimate communication" might be defined as the fulfillment of the high-technology dream—to have all information and entertainment on the Earth instantly available to all people. This media utopia would include real sounds, images, smells, and other sensory stimuli of the highest quality transmitted to each individual for their selection, editing, storage, or replay. Moreover, all people could communicate with all others efficiently, cheaply, and instantly employing all senses over the information superhighway.

For the Indigenous Peoples, "ultimate" or ideal communication would have been based on different values. For most, the ideal would have been to *commune with all life* (not to communicate with all "significant" people) with the *least* technology (not the most) with the greatest sensitivity to the Great Spirit's patterns.

To be sure, tribal goals seemed to vary with tribal needs. Throughout the history of Indigenous Peoples, three primary and often overlapping needs seem to have developed: (1) survival, (2) success, and (3) spiritual fulfillment. Endangered tribes seeking simply to survive would have different goals for communication than more stable tribes seeking to become successful (i.e., comfortable, prosperous, victorious, or at peace, depending on their values). The goal of spiritual fulfillment might overlap with survival or notions of success, or it might be the unequivocal prerequisite for both.

In any event, each of the three types of tribe would view ultimate communication in different terms. Survival-oriented tribes sought practical forms of communication. The scout who could distinguish specific animals from enemy scouts from three miles away was far more valuable than a scout who could only perceive vague movements at two miles. The farmer who could discern advancing locusts or rabbits could compete favorably with his less perceptive counterparts. For the *survival*-oriented tribes, "ultimate" communication included such forms as enhancing the senses; developing the technologies of warning such as smoke signals, long-distance drums, cup and saucer rocks, and Native "scarecrows;" heightening sensitivity to weather conditions; anticipating predator behavior; and understanding the communication and strategies of rival tribes.

*Success*-oriented tribes might emphasize a different approach. Having minimized danger, they could relax and enjoy more entertaining and educational modes of communication. More time for storytelling, crafting jewelry and clothing, creating ceremony and song meant an emphasis on internal, nourishing communication. Elements of vanity and competition could become more prominent: leaders or suitors who desired the "most" attractive headdress, face painting, tattoo, or walking stick had time to improve their "image."

When food was bountiful, larger families could be supported, so educational communication within the extended family, military induction societies, "novitiate" hunting parties, and medicine hogan apprenticeships became more commonplace. Finally, *success*-oriented societies could upgrade their material, social, and marital opportunities through outreach or intratribal communication. Trading parties, mass ceremonies, multitribe potlatch events, and well-attended weddings demanded new forms of group communication, trading protocol, intertribal sign language, and an increasing need for translators.

A major difference in the *spiritual* communication of specific tribes depended on whether they were motivated primarily by survival or success. Tribes seeking to survive needed boons from the gods: much of their prayer and ceremony, like a child's requests of "Santa Claus," demanded gifts—favorable weather, victory in battle, abundant crops, or deliverance from a plague or plight. While successful tribes might also maintain these traditions, they favored a different type of dialogue with the Creator(s)—ceremonies of thankfulness, celebration, and creation might be more abundant, and there would be more time for consecrating one's life through rites of passage and other commitment rituals.

A truly spiritual tribe maintained a spirit of rejoicing and thanksgiving no matter what their circumstances. Even if survival were threatened or success jeopardized, they sustained reverence and consistent worship events. Cynics may argue that this innocent state was maintained because worship formed the ultimate form of protection, hence it was in the Native's self-interest to be thankful as a bridge to future survival and success. But more traditional people have countered this argument with a much simpler perspective: "One always has the same respectful attitude toward the Gods," says Sun Bear, "not so they *will* help you, but rather because they already have. You owe your existence, your breath, and all your pleasures to them already—so why not give thanks and celebrate, no matter what?" (interview, 2/28/88).

Thus it is not surprising to discover that the most common forms of Native spiritual communication convey thankfulness. Prayer, song, chant, dance, silence, communion, art, and thought often exist for no other reason. Similarly, there is a common *rule* of Native spiritual communication: reply to the gods. If the gods had spoken to man through creation, through messages, through lightning and the wind, it was unthinkable not to reply. The secondary intertribal rules of communication considered earlier were peripheral relative to this central command: Divine communication requires a response. The responses—vision quests, animal sacrifices, food offerings, prolonged silence fasts, marathon chants, human sacrifices, songs of praise—were diverse.

If the gods seemed creative, the natural response was thankfulness, repayment, and rejoicing. If the gods seemed destructive or punitive, for example, through volcanoes and earthquakes, the natural response was fearful appeasement, such as through offerings, fasting, and sacrifices. Such communication was usually based on a sense of "separateness" from the gods. If the gods seemed distant, they needed to be contacted for favors or by ceremonial "thank you" notes. "Ultimate communication" was a different state entirely. Those Indigenous People who practiced it did not use communication to *search* for the gods, but rather used it when fully identified with them. Such Kahunas (Hawaiian priests) carried the aura of *being,* or *being among* gods and goddesses.

Ultimate communication revealed different dimensions when such individuals felt unified with the Great Spirit. Consider this passage about the Campa people:

*Earth once spoke to humans and animals at the beginning of creation. According to the Campa of Eastern Peru, Earth spoke infrequently and slowly, using a limited scale of Tones: She ceased speaking after she became fed up with the rotting flesh of cadavers buried in her. (Sullivan 1985, 406)*

In the numerous accounts of the Earth speaking to humans and vice versa, it seems apparent that only those who reached a truly selfless state heard the Earth.

Such selflessness, or attainment of a "higher" identity transcending or dissolving personhood, allowed many Aboriginals to feel at one with the earth, the stars, and the elements. Rather than being foreign or foreboding, the "universe," often perceived as giant animals, plants, or spirits in the sky, became "home." Indeed, Richard Heinberg suggested that for the Aboriginal fully at home with the universe, ultimate communication took on truly cosmic proportions: "If communication comes from the core of one's being, then it amounts to the universe being conscious and talking to itself . . . one would think the universe would be very happy to talk to itself clearly" (interview, 8/11/90).

A common assumption among those aspiring to higher communication was that a divine "vision" alone was insufficient. For a higher experience to occur, the receiver of that vision must put it into practice. In Black Elk's words, "A man who has a vision is not able to use the power of it until after he has performed the vision of it on earth for people to see" (1961, 33). Consequently, if a god gave you an idea or vision to further enlighten or assist your people, it was the application of the vision that would reveal its true meaning. At another level, what was meant was, until Divine vision is taken to be *instruction,* its meaning will not be clear. In following the *instruction,* a new meaning would arrive from implementing the vision.

Thus communications from a deity often required followup labor that revealed deeper communication on completion of the task. For example, if a vision inspired one to build an instrument, the sound of the instrument could not be heard prior to completion of the task. The sound of the instrument might be taken as the real message communicated by the God, not the original vision that inspired one to build the instrument. Ultimate communication, then, included the "payoff" message, not just the initial command.

In this sense ultimate spiritual communication is what is learned through *applied* spiritual living, rather than the imparting of isolated scriptures and omens. This is one reason elders were frequently revered: their actions were born out of decades of application of the Gods' instructions; they could be trusted not to merely speak theory or to practice religious mimicry. At their best, the elders were only interested in what was genuine, effective, and truly divine.

Ultimate communication suggested oneness with the Creator. Rather than waiting for the Great Spirit to provide healing, the Native doctor became a God, bringing the forces of creation to bear on the forces of destruction or illness. Curtis noted that "in nearly every Indian myth the creator sings things into life" (1987); similarly, in nearly every Indigenous society the human creator (medicine man, doctor, shaman, or priest) sang things into health.

Not only the wounded person but also the dying bird, spruce, or grasshopper might receive the singer's healing magic. Although the healing ceremony was not always successful in curing the patient, it usually provided those attending with a strong sensing of divine presence.

There will be many who doubt the very notion of "ultimate communication." After all, if humans have evolved up the Darwinian or Spencerian ladder, ultimate communication has not yet been attained. Indeed, we seem to be evolving toward subtle, yet more powerful, technologies of sound and image replication than ever before. Perhaps none of these technologies will be the penultimate, but rather another harbinger of greater inventions still to come.

However, if our species has *devolved* from gods to destroyers of the Earth, as suggested in Aboriginal myth, ultimate communication may have, in some or many ways, already been attained in ancient days. If the residual memory of oral societies, as translated into most creation stories and myths, points toward true North, then higher means of communicating existed prior to the "flood," whether symbolic or actual, mentioned in most ancient literatures.

Nor is it difficult to project an antediluvian time of ultimate communication based on some of the phrases of the elders I have heard: "a time before lying;" "the age of long-distance speaking and listening;" "the era when we walked and talked among the animals;" "before the Gods went away and stopped talking to us;" "when there was no need for words;" "when each person had his own unique instrument;" "when our ceremonies were real, not symbols;" "when First Man and First Woman spoke as one;" "when silence created all sounds and pictures;" "when the great hunter could see everywhere and hear a feather drop across the lake;" "when we all sang together the songs we never had to learn;" "before forked tongue."

There can be no knowing exactly what occurred thousands or even hundreds of years ago. The kindred phrases and uncritical discussion above only hint at a possible ancient world of unadulterated spiritual communication. Outside Native circles, such a world seems distant, clouded, and based on minuscule *written* evidence. Indeed, skeptics accurately point out that the word "utopia" means "nowhere" and that "nowhere" is the only place "ultimate communication" might ever have existed. To romanticize the past, it is argued, can only raise false standards for the future and reinforce disillusionment with the present.

Nevertheless, the rejoinder of many Native People would be, "You have taken away everything else from us. Do not also seek to take from us our legacy, our divine origins, our mythic memories." Moreover, many paradigms and facets of knowledge, from the concept of an Earth-centered universe, or of a flat earth, to the assumption that bleeding the patient would bring health, have proven mistaken. Who can assert with absolute authority that the theory of evolutionary biology will be the exception that, by virtue of its accuracy, proves that rule?

For centuries literate societies have demanded that nonliterate or tribal peoples learn from their superior system based on linear, logical, literate communication. In the spirit of fairness, ethics, and reciprocity, is it not time that the guests also learn from the oral, mythic, and spiritual heritage of their hosts? Are there Aboriginal values, ethics, and communication forms and practices from which others might learn?

## Learning from the Hosts

While neither all literate nor all oral societies are alike or static, much may be learned by perceiving how the two groups differ. Different societies, cultures, and individuals may discover from each other. Given the contrasts between traditional tribal and modern urban communication, the list below suggests what the latter society might learn from the former.

1. **Individual stillness:** being still until one has meaningful words to utter could contribute to reducing many sources of modern anxiety—noise pollution, superficial communication, urban babble, talk radio, and the increasing inability to hear natural sounds.

2. **Group stillness:** silence prior to and during important meet-ings—until an atmosphere of genuine dialogue is developed —could be useful to parliaments, congresses, town councils, conventions, and similar gatherings known for endless rhetor-ical debate, filibuster, repetitive platitudes, and grandstanding.

3. **Full-spectrum listening:** hearing the voices of the environ-ment—whether the painful cries of species being eliminated, the forests being amputated, or earthquakes and other natural outcries—has never been more important. Similarly, listen-ing to the heart, motivation, and needs of the speaker is often more valuable than just hearing the surface message.

4. **Respect:** in an age of intense confrontation, criticism, blame, name-calling, and accusation, the Native call to respect—for one's listener or audience, for the speaker or artist, for one's partner in dialogue, for all life and a greater context—would be refreshing and healthy.

5. **Containment:** when press leaks, electronic eavesdropping, invasion of privacy, and larger-than-life scandals are escalat-ing, it may be wise to consider Native dictums such as "Never say more than you know," "Never tell all that you know," and "Keep what is sacred among the sacred."

6. **Protection of reputation:** as an increase in the volume of libel suits and character assassinations has been noted in this century, the notion of "protection of reputation" is instructive. Refraining from accusation without necessity, from bringing charges without evidence, and from defa-mation without reflection could be helpful. Indeed, many Natives would urge an even more positive approach, such as seeing the divine spirit within each person and stressing pos-itive traits.

7. **Group celebration:** As an upbeat counterbalance to the neg-ative communication listed above, a redirected emphasis on

group celebration, such as tribal dances and community song, would be at least therapeutic and at most highly generative.

8. **Healing communication:** the shaman's communication—singing, marathon dance, chant, blowing of water, touching the patient, wound massage—seems unsophisticated in an age of miracle drugs and high tech treatment. However, as research reveals how much illness is psychosomatic and involves healing of identity, heart, self-esteem, balance, mind, and "soul," therapies involving the arts, relaxation, change of atmosphere, touch, and spirituality are proving more widespread and, in some cases, more effective. What the physician communicates to the patient subconsciously—for example, care, compassion, gentleness, understanding, and assurance—is also important.

9. **Subculture ceremony:** daily sweat lodge singing and storytelling, whether among men, women, or mixed adults, foster camaraderie often lacking in urban society. Core creative communication, whether within the rites of passage of women with girls, men with boys, or women with men, increases community bonding and mature identity.

10. **Realism:** in an age of endless exaggeration, such as in tabloid television or scandal sheets, an emphasis on avoiding gossip and distortion, in favor of laconic exactness, is helpful.

11. **Communion:** sensitivity to all levels of life and to full communication opens the door for alienated people to return to more understanding, fuller lives, integration within their larger context, spiritual fulfillment, and the dissolution of anomie. No society has had more marriage counseling, arbitrators, negotiation specialists, and communication workshops than those societies that superimposed their communication practices on Natives. Communion, in its many levels, settings, and forms, is a profound alternative.

12. **Truthfulness:** no one may claim to know or tell all truth given each person's subjective interpretation and beliefs about the nature of truth. Nevertheless, being *truthful,* that is, being true to the truth as best one knows it, is a Native trait that could help dissolve distrust, inaccuracy, and animosity. Whether or not there was a time before deception, a sustained commitment to truthfulness not only reverses the tendencies provoked by the "forked tongue" but also provides a sacred bond among individuals and between the two cultures.

## Conclusion

I have always appreciated those books that left conclusions to the reader. Most Native societies would have avoided pedantic proselytizing and propagandistic approaches to communication. So shall I. In a balanced approach there are no extreme evils or supreme goods. Even General Custer must have communicated effectively in some moments and even the most powerful kahuna, shaman, or chief must have made slips of the tongue. Oral and literate peoples may reciprocally learn from each other without superiority or inferiority complexes.

However, most learning and listening thus far has been imposed by the guest cultures on their hosts. To restore a balanced approach, it is necessary to take a stand. Clearly, that stand states that the myriad Native approaches to communication have been widely misunderstood and ought to be better understood. Indigenous Peoples have been immersed in and converted to foreign cultures without reciprocity or representation. Not only are tribal views valid, they are valuable. Not only are Native approaches wise, but wise approaches are Native to us all when we recall a common ancestry.

If communion is prerequisite to effective communication, it

could be useful for those who chose to experience and express communion. If ceremony and celebration strengthen the community, it could be both practical and nourishing to employ both on a voluntary basis. *If* we have devolved rather than evolved, how would we "remember" higher levels of communication without being open-minded and reflective? If Aboriginal communication practices and values enhance social continuity and spiritual depth, why should they be censored or censured?

It is a Western tradition to complete a book with a clever conclusion, a recommendation for further research, or a summary of the chapters. Such has been my habit. However, it was a Native custom to conclude lengthy deliberations with sacred ceremony of acknowledgment of the Great Spirit and the elders. To honor my many Native friends and associates who have given their heritage and insights to this text, I wish to conclude these thoughts with such acknowledgment.

It is not the author's seeming wit or wisdom that needs to impress. Rather it is the dignified articulation by millions of Aboriginal colleagues that is worthy of recognition. They in turn would give credit to the many animals, plants, stars, waves, winds, thoughts, songs, and spirits who created their world and who are increasingly silenced by the sound of the bulldozer and the broadcast. If these words may in some way undergird the reversal of that muzzling process, then both the Great Spirit and the great spirit of Indigenous People will be acknowledged.

# Epilogue

The open hand of the American Indian presented to a stranger who in turn displays an open hand indicates neither man carries a weapon. Therefore, it is a sign of peace. This sign is common and understood by societies around the world.

When the lion is not hunting all who observe him know this by the attitude of his walk and composure. He will stroll by his traditional quarry eliciting from them occasional nervous glances as they go about their grazing. This is communicated by body language for the quarry. It is life and death. It is truth.

The oldest form of communication between human beings is sign language and could also be the difference between life and death. Sign language is still used today. Perhaps you have experienced it yourself, finding yourself in a different country with a language you don't understand. You are forced to revert to sign language to obtain directions or help. Sight is essential to sign language and must be interpreted by the viewer. For the animal world these body attitudes are constant and truthful. For human beings there can be and is an ambiguity. Societies of man differ. The contrast between western society and Indigenous Peoples of the western hemisphere is the obvious one in America — "Honest Injun" for American Indians and "Get it in writing" for the American people.

The magnificent speeches and statements by American Indian leaders and people are legendary for their ethical and moral content. These statements are based upon cultures that place the spoken word at the epitome of honor and commitment. The speaker assumes that the receiver of his words has the same ethics and societal standards—here is where communications failed the Indian and continues to fail American society. Adding to the problem is the fact that moral and ethical standards have changed since the time of Benjamin Franklin, George Washington, and Thomas Jefferson. From the time the English landed at Plymouth to their evolution into an American democratic society, they were inspired by the Iroquois' great league of peace, and they reached a plateau of democracy that inspired other nations to form democratic governments. The Continental Congress was as close to American Indian free society as they would get.

However, during the development of the U.S. Constitution, the Founding Fathers could not give up slavery, nor would they give the new government a "one man-one vote" standard. They elected to develop the "electoral" state vote, which can and has overturned a popular election. Finally, they did not recognize women as equal partners in life or government. These flaws were and are costly. Consider the Civil War and 371 broken Indian treaties. These flaws helped to engender a national arrogance of racism that culminated in a theory called "Manifest Destiny" in 1843.

It is my opinion that to begin to lie to others you must first lie to yourself to the point that the lie becomes your rationale for reality.

Today, American society is certainly reaching another plateau of credibility. There is a gap of cynicism growing between American people and the government on all levels. People just don't believe politicians anymore. George Orwell's description of "doublespeak" in his classic book, *1984*, is here now. People are not being told the truth. In U.S. Government "doublespeak," the word "pre-emptive strike" means a military attack launched without warning. Advertising has perfected the technique of "double-speak" and the art of misleading. Tobacco industry leaders have openly lied not only to the public but also to the Congress of the United States.

Further, there is distrust, anger, and fear between the working class and big business. Something is drastically wrong when corporations and businesses are "down-sized" by firing their personnel. Then business reaches out to cheaper sources of labor and resources. At the same time "down-sizing" occurs, their stock prices go up—the benefit is all for the "owners," the stockholders. American Government and business had a hard time bringing themselves even to raise the minimum wage. People were told by Congressional House leader Newt Gingrich that raising the minimum wage would be bad for them and they would lose jobs.

We are in strange times when poor peoples' wages are frozen at the same level for over ten years and individual fortunes are going through the roof. There is a widening gap between the haves and the have-nots. A recent study of this phenomenon by the *New York Times* reported: "Labor Department statistics show that more than thirty-six million jobs were eliminated between 1970 and 1993, and an analysis by the *New York Times* puts the number at forty-three million through 1995. Many of the jobs would disappear in any age, when a store closes or an old product like the typewriter yields to a new one like the computer. What distinguishes this age are three phenomena: white collar workers are big victims; large corporations now account for many of the layoffs; and a large percentage of the jobs are lost to 'outsourcing' —contracting out work to another company, usually within the United States."

Far more jobs are being added than lost. But many of the new jobs are in small companies that offer scant benefits and less pay, and many are part time positions with no benefits at all. Often the laid-off get only temporary work, tackling tasks once performed by fulltimers. This country's largest employer, renting out 767,000 substitute workers each year, is Manpower, Inc., the temporary help agency. Louis Uchitelle and N. R. Kleinfield asked in the *New York Times,* Sunday, March 5, 1996, "What does it mean to the working man when the largest employer in the country is a temporary help agency?"

What does "downsizing" mean? What does "outsourcing" mean? It comes down to "doublespeak" in western society. How do we become a truthful society when political and business leaders fail to lead in that direction? Economics and "development" are the leading forces in the world today. Profit is the god, and people are the resource. There is little long-term thinking when market forces and information or Wall Street are measured in milliseconds.

*A Time Before Deception* explores perspectives that cannot be ignored in developing the long-term thinking and ethical communication necessary to solve the grave problems facing western society today.

American Indians say that we are responsible for the well-being of the seventh generation coming out. American Indians are no longer in charge of North America. That is your responsibility now. It is your question to answer. What is the future of human beings on earth? That judgment will be made seven generations from now.

**Oren Lyons**
Chief, Onondaga Nation
Haudensaunee

# Appendix:
# A Word
# about Methods

## Background

This book deliberately expands the boundaries of critical studies out of respect for the epistemology, property rights, and hermeneutics of Indigenous Peoples. Some years ago I might have written this by applying semiology, critical theory, or some other methodology "foreign" to Indigenous Peoples. After living with Native Americans, Hawaiians, and Native Canadians, I now understand why they consider such scholarship a form of theft and serious misrepresentation.

In recent years, controversies have arisen about the ownership of Native American, Aboriginal, and other indigenous relics, bones, and fossils found within or near Native reservations. Indigenous Peoples have claimed that such remains are sacred, belong to the Earth, carry various spirits or residual energy, or simply that they are "Indian" property. U.S., Australian, Canadian, and other governments or scientists have often made competing claims that the remains belong to the government, to science, or to humanity at large.

It is not widely known that a similar debate occurs surrounding related scholarship. Although the anthropologist, ethnog-

**195**

rapher, archaeologist—or, in my case, communication scholar—feels entitled to study any culture with any methodology, the peoples studied often feel invaded, misunderstood, decontextualized, even raped of meaning. Moreover, when outsiders obtain "native" knowledge or secrets and use them for a profit through external publications, Indigenous People often feel that sacred or innate knowledge has been stolen from its context by thieves and profiteers. In many cases, the peoples studied never see the final, if any, draft of the publications, let alone any of the profits.

In the literature of Agrawal, Brislin, Doob, and others on cross-cultural studies, the view of the "insider" has been called the "emic" (as in endemic) approach, while "outsider" (i.e., anthropological, Western) methods have been named the "etic" approach. To be fair to the Indigenous People, with whom I visited and lived, I have chosen to use, whenever possible, the "emic" (insider) approach. That is, there is no attempt to analyze the tribal mode of communication with foreign methodologies and thus ravish them of their larger world order. In that sense this is a work of intercession or translation in which in my primitive way (I am not Aboriginal), I endeavor to present the Native world of communication in ways that they have already approved as respectful and comprehending of their *umwelt*.

Just as a traditional tributary of our Western critical scholarship might be entitled "appreciation"—as in film, music, and art *appreciation* classes—the closest to critical studies one finds among ancient Native wisdom most resembles our methods of *appreciation*. That is, the attempt to critically understand the work communicated is not through analysis and nomenclature but rather through a thorough appreciation of the culture, techniques, mindset, environment, and (for Indigenous Peoples) the spiritual whole in which it is embedded.

In honoring that approach, this work attempts to understand Indigenous communication within its own terms. Other methods of criticism might have been applied to Native knowledge, and indeed have been by other authors. But in such cases, Aboriginal wisdom is not imparted, but rather something else—an interpretation that neuters, fragments, and ultimately destroys Native meaning.

While I do not abandon Western analysis (see my other publications for various Eurocentric methods), in this book, I honor the insider's perspective. Whenever possible, I assume that we, the imported "guests," have much to learn from the authentic—albeit immigrated—tribal nations. Although in most Native languages there is no word for "communication" or for "ethics," there is what could be called a culturally inculcated "communication ethic" that broadens our own options and learning.

In that regard, this essay seems to present the Native communication ethic and overworld uncritically. However, at another level, which is critical, both the book and the Aboriginal introduce a way of understanding what is beneath the surface of the visible realm of our communication interaction.

## The Shuswap

Much of my efforts have been in communication ethics. Of great importance are the moral rules that determine how a society communicates. Who may speak to whom? About what? How loudly? With how much freedom or censorship? To the point of damaging reputation? By invading privacy? In an age and society that decry increasing noise pollution, hype, deceptive advertising, infotainment, oversexed and violent media messages, slick and superficial conversation, and hollow noncommunication ethics in general, can we learn about communication ethics from earlier, quieter, possibly wiser ancestors?

In the winter of 1991 I set out for central British Columbia to pose related questions to two bands of Native Canadian Shuswap people living on reserves hundreds of miles from cities. My friend Dorothy Hughes who lived in 100 Mile House between the Canim Lake and Alkali Lake Shuswap bands introduced me to her old friends at the Canim Lake and at the Alkali Lake Shuswap Reserves. During the spring and earlier summer I visited and occasionally lived at the reserves and interviewed elders and - community leaders.

Two questions motivated my research: "What were the early forms and ethical rules of Shuswap communication?" and "What might we (modern non-Shuswap observers) learn from these earlier customs and ethics?"

My own ethics were scrutinized in this process. Was I simply trying to take valuable information from an Indigenous group or was I willing to give in return? At their request, I was happy to give talks, to teach band members to conduct research themselves, to give a workshop, to participate in the local culture (sweathouse, ceremonial singing and dancing, building and sleeping in a tepee, and so forth), to copyright and share my research for Native use, and to videotape then donate tapes of interviews with specific elders. I was also delighted to donate toward scholarships for young Natives and provide other gifts without being nudged. I sought to participate openly in the community as a friend and equal based on the Shuswap values of respect and reciprocity rather than import foreign values and a hidden agenda.

## METHODS: AMONG THE SHUSWAP

At Canim Lake Reserve ten elders, ages 56 to 75, and nine community leaders with historical or cultural expertise, ages 30 to 62, were interviewed about the "old ways" of Shuswap communication. Some of these had been educated in the Roman Catholic mission schools while others were educated primarily by their Shuswap parents. Thus questions had to be devised to distinguish old Shuswap traditions from cultural norms implanted by the mission schools. As an informal control group, nine Alkali Lake residents—six elders and three community cultural leaders —were interviewed. The six elders, ages 62 to 100, and three others, ages 43 to 52, had been raised on or near the Alkali Lake Reserve.

Shuswap elders are neither elected nor appointed but rather perceived by unspoken consensus. They are men and women old enough to be grandparents, who serve as highly revered consultants to the community, and are often survived by large numbers of children and grandchildren who comprise a key component of the community mainstream.

Approximately 80 percent of the Canim Lake elders and 50 percent of the Alkali Lake elders were interviewed. Of these approximately two-thirds were women, a proportion in keeping with the higher numbers of senior Shuswap women. At Canim Lake an attempt was made to interview all elders—those who were not interviewed were either unavailable or consistently missed appointments (a relatively small number). Due to the extraordinary courtesy and hospitality of the Canim Lake community leaders, I was also invited to attend a meeting of the elders and brief them on the purpose of the research.

All of those interviewed were asked twenty-nine standardized questions in English. Twenty interviews were conducted in the homes of those questioned while the other nine occurred in or near reserve band offices or schools. During most interviews, a band liaison traveled with me to learn research techniques and to help with occasional translation or rephrasing a question.

Interviews typically lasted sixty to ninety minutes and were conducted with a sense of naturalness in or as if in one's living room. However, it was agreed that all background media (TV or radio), loud children, or similar distractions would be distanced or softened to focus on the interview. Often a question would inspire thought but not an immediate answer, so we would return to it later.

The elders interviewed and their age at the time of the interview are listed below:

| CANIM LAKE | ALKALI LAKE |
|---|---|
| Joe Archie (68) | Amelia Johnson (79) |
| Dora Archie (66) | Lily Squinahan (79) |
| Eddie Dixon (73) | Hazel Johnson (62) |
| Ike Daniels (59) | Ellen Robbins (62) |
| Jim Frank (56) | Mahdi Spahan (100) |
| Mary Agnes Frank (56) | via Ellen Robbins |
| Cecelia Bob (75) | Laura Harry (71) |
| Norman Bob (59) | |
| May Dixon (71) | |
| Rita Charlie (67) | |

Other band members interviewed in 1991 were:

| CANIM LAKE | ALKALI LAKE |
|---|---|
| Antoinette Archie | Juliana Johnson |
| Sheila Dick | Fred Johnson |
| Elizabeth Pete | Johnny Johnson |

Mary Alice Danaher (non-Native)
Alana Dixon
Gary Emile
Charlotte Christopher
Elsie Theodore
Mark Boyce (part-time resident at Canim Lake)
Fred Christopher

# The Diné

In August 1990, I sojourned to northeastern Arizona to live at the Rock Point Reservation. Thanks to the highly respected reputation of my friend Eleanor Velarde, a teacher at the Rock Point Community School, I became a guest who was welcomed by several of her Native friends. A letter I wrote to the tribal council requested permission to conduct research at Rock Point. Such a letter was far more than a formality since many rapacious and insensitive researchers have often given a bad name to visiting "scholars."

Earlier that year as a guest scholar at Harvard I had reviewed the "external" literature about the Navajo. On arrival at Rock Point I immediately reviewed the "internal" (written by Native literature about Diné, much of which is housed at the library of the Rock Point Community School or owned by community leaders and teachers.

Using the interviewing methods and questions described above, I interviewed twenty-seven community elders, leaders, and teachers, most of whom were recommended by Eleanor Velarde or by a Diné friend and translator, Rex Lee Jim. Since Rex Lee Jim had been first reared and educated as a Diné at Rock Point, then as a cosmopolitan at Princeton University, he was an excellent translator, not only of languages but also of cultures and mental frames.

As with the Shuswap, I approached my Rock Point visit with an attitude of provision rather than acquisition. On discovering that it was considered both customary and ethical for researchers to pay those interviewed, I weighed the implications and decided to pay the customary $10 per interview, in most cases with money, in others with food. To pay for interviews creates the potential problem that participants will be more likely to say what they think you want to hear. So it was necessary to stress that candor, rather than trying to fulfill expectations, characterized a successful interview.

As with the Shuswap, I used a four step outer-to-inner approach:

1. studying the outer (written by non-Natives) literature and working with outside experts;
2. being oriented to the inner culture by an "outside insider" (in this case, Eleanor Velarde), that is, someone who lives within the Diné culture but who was originally from my culture and thus could translate many, but not all, cultural differences into my language and cultural frame;
3. being further oriented by an "inside outsider" (in this case, Rex Lee Jim), that is, by an insider who also was educated within the outsider's language, culture, and approach. Rex Lee Jim had grown up at Rock Point but had attended Princeton;
4. being informed by "total insiders," those who, as the most authentic Diné, speak only the Native language, are the least known and influenced by outsiders, and have seldom, if ever, traveled beyond Diné land.

Despite this approach, I encountered many methodological challenges, which will only be outlined below. Many of these have also been encountered or discussed by Zolbred, Witherspoon, Kluckhohn, and numerous others living among or visiting the Diné:

1. All oral literature, like interviewing, relies on memory. When asking questions of senior citizens about their childhood memories of the culture of their elders, and when reading or hearing Native myths that were orally transmitted for generations, how can one determine the relative accuracy, validity, and reliability of what is reported?

2. Translation from one language into another is also from one rhythm, *weltanschauung,* poetic, *stimmung,* lifestyle, and frame of reference into another. Is such translation or interpretation ever fully evocative, or representative of the full range of subtexts within a text?

3. What is meant to be spoken in an oral culture has very different rules than what is meant to be written in other societies (see introduction and chapters 3, 4). Outsiders are never sure of what is *not* being spoken, or withheld.

4. In some Native societies, interviewees are told, "Tell the white man whatever he wants to hear so he will leave." In others they are told, "Do not say things which might damage the reputation of our people." In some tribes, the amount of money interviewees are paid may influence their openness or empathy toward the interviewer and his or her expectations. In such conditions, how may absolute candor be guaranteed?

5. The researcher, no matter how scientific (and often because he or she *is* scientific), is constantly hearing interviews and reading literature through a series of subjective cultural, professional, academic, and other filters.

6. As mentioned in chapter 3, what is orally reported cannot be extracted from a larger, organic whole. However, to organize and write down observations is necessarily to decontextualize, fragment, and Westernize the interviews and people who grant them.

7. As Innis and others have articulated, writing itself brings a specific bias of linearity, syntax, and edited regimentation to thought. Written ideas may be vastly different than the consciousness of the original speaker, or from that same thought when presented through another communication medium.

8. Research itself is inherently selective, analytic, deductive, and patterned. By reshaping knowledge, the research may be partly

or fully misrepresenting culture and isolating cerebral drop-
lets from the larger flow that brought them forth.

9. Natives often insist that one will never understand their internal ambience and subtleties without living among them a
lifetime, or at least twenty years or so. Conversely, most of us
conducting research have lived twenty years, if not most of a
lifetime, at distant universities, institutes, and cities.

Realizing that these and many other differences and difficul-
ties existed, I (1) accepted that my research would be astigmatic
no matter what steps I took; (2) nevertheless took steps to mini-
mize the astigmatism by living on the reservation, visiting hogans
distant from the central community, inviting the local folk to
help me see through their eyes, and studying their "internal"
archives; (3) devised uniform questions at the beginning of
interviews to test the memory and reliability of those interviewed;
and (4) in general, blended proven research methods with Diné
wisdom about the limitation of research in understanding their
views. The methodological discussions of previous researchers,
such as Zolbred and Leighton, also proved valuable.

Those interviewed at the Rock Point Reservation in northeastern Arizona were asked about the old ways of communicating
prior to outside encroachment. All were asked about their earliest
memories and the most ancient stories and memories told them
by their elders and the elders' elders. Although there seem to be
no surviving Diné totally uninfluenced by America's government
or Hispanic conqueror and other immigrants, I endeavored to
find those least encumbered by American culture as well as those
most encumbered, that is, those fully educated in the U.S. system
who could thus compare the two cultures and mindsets. Within
the latter category, I also interviewed two white educators, Dan
McLaughlin and Clyde Duncan, who had lived with the Diné at

length and, in Duncan's case, married into the Diné community. These experiences gave them a unique basis for empathy and comparison.

The Diné interviewed ranged from such senior respected leaders as Thomas Littleben, age 70, to such junior leaders as Princeton-educated Rex Lee Jim, age 26. More elder than younger people, and more permanent than cosmopolitan (traveled) residents were chosen. Slightly fewer women than men were interviewed, although equal numbers would have been preferred.

Some of those interviewed preferred to be anonymous (referred to in Chapter 5 as "an educator," or a "shepherd" or similar), and most preferred to have their English name listed. Out of deep respect for my Rock Point associates, I have honored all requests for confidentiality, anonymity, privacy, deferred questions, and the limits to sacred areas of discussion.

# References

Abler, Thomas, and Sally Weaver. *A Canadian Indian Bibliography.* Toronto: University of Toronto Press, 1974.

Abrahams, R. "A Modern Witch-Hunt among the Lango of Uganda." *Cambridge Anthropology* 10, no. 1 (1985): 32–44.

Agar, Michael. *The Professional Stranger: An Informal Introduction to Ethnography.* New York: Academic Press, 1980.

Ainsworth, Nancy. "The Cultural Shaping of Oral Discourse." *Theory into Practice* 23, no. 2 (Spring 1984): 132–137.

Alisjahbana, Sutan Takdir. *Values as Integrating Forces in Personality, Society and Culture: Essays of A New Anthology.* Kuala Lumpur: Malaya University Press, 1974.

Amoss, Pamela. *Coast Salish Spirit Dancing: The Survival of an Ancestral Religion.* Seattle: University of Washington Press, 1978.

Anderson, Terence R. "The Right to Make Our Own Mistakes," *Touchstone* 2, no. 2 (May 1984): 29–43.

Appell, George N. *Ethical Dilemmas in Anthropological Inquiry: A Case Book.* Los Angeles: Crossroads Press, 1978.

Arberry, Arthur J. *The Koran Interpreted.* New York: Macmillan, 1955.

Archie, Antoinette. Canim Lake Band, May and June 1991. Interview.

Archie, Dora. Canim Lake Band, April and May 1991. Interview.

Archie, Joe. Canim Lake Band, April and May 1992. Interview.

Arden, Harvey, and Steve Wall. *Wisdom Keepers: Meetings with Native American Spiritual Elders.* Hillsboro, Ore.: Beyond Words Publishers, 1991.

Ardener, S. "The Comparative Study of Rotating Credit Associations." *Journal of the Royal Anthropological Institute* 94: 210–229.

Arno, Andrew. *The World of Talk on a Fijian Island.* Norwood, N.J.: Ablex, 1993.

Ashmore, Wendy, and Robert J. Sharer. *Discovering our Past: A Brief Introduction to Archaeology.* Mountain View, Calif.: Mayfield, 1988.

Astrov, Margaret. "The Concept of Motion as the Psychological Leitmotif of Navajo Life and Literature." *Journal of American Folklore* 63 (1950): 45–56.

Atrigg, Helen Brown. *"History and Economic Development of Shuswap Area."* M.A. thesis, Department of History, University of British Columbia, 1964.

Baal, Jan van. *Man's Quest for Partnership: The Anthropological Foundations of Ethics and Religion.* Assen, the Netherlands: Van Gorcum, 1981.

_____. *Symbols for Communication: An Introduction to the Anthropological Study of Religion.* Assen: Van Gorcum, 1971.

Bagshawe, F. J. "The Peoples of the Happy Valley (East Africa)." "The Aboriginal Races of Kondoa Irangi, Part II, The Kangeju." *Journal of the African Society* 24, no. 94 (January 1925): 117–130.

Barfield, Owen. *Poetic Diction: A Study in Meaning.* 3d ed. Middletown, Conn.: Wesleyan University Press, 1973.

_____. *Worlds Apart: A Dialogue of the 1960s.* Middletown, Conn.: Wesleyan University Press, 1960.

Barlow, S. M. *Light Is Sown.* Chicago: Moody Press, 1956.

Barnett, Homer. *The Coast Salish of British Columbia.* Eugene: University of Oregon Press, 1955.

Barney, Ralph, and John Maestas. "Comparisons of Information Sources and Media Usage Among On-and-Off Members of the Navajo Tribe." Paper presented at Western Social Science Association Annual Conference, Albuquerque, New Mexico, 1989.

_____. "Information Sources and Attitude Differences among On-And-Off Members of the Navajo Tribe." Paper presented at Western Social Science Association Annual Conference, Albuquerque, New Mexico, 1989.

Barroso, Porfirio Ahenjo. *Fundamentos Deontológicos de las Ciencias de la Información.* Barcelona, Spain: Editorial Mitre, 1985.

Barsh, Russel Lawrence. "Are Anthropologists Hazardous to Indians' Health?" *Journal of Ethnic Studies* 15, no. 4 (Winter 1988): 1–3 8.

Bateson, Gregory. *Steps to an Ecology of Mind.* New York: Ballantine Books, 1972.

Beane, Wendell Charles. *Myth, Cult and Symbols in Sakta Hinduism: A Study of the Indian Mother Goddess.* Leiden: Brill, 1977.

Beck, Peggy V. *The Sacred: Ways of Knowledge, Sources of Life.* Tsaile, Ariz.: Navajo Community College, 1977.

Bell, Diane. "Working with Women: Aboriginal Religion." Paper delivered at the Workshop on Primal Spirituality, East-West Center, Institute of Culture and Communication, University of Hawaii-Manoa, January 15, 1991.

_____. Honolulu, East–West Center, January 1991. Interview.

Berendt, Joachim Ernst. *Nada Brahma, The World Is Sound: Music and the Landscape of Consciousness.* 1st U.S. ed. Rochester, Vt: Destiny Books, 1987.

Berndt, Ronald M. , ed. *Australian Aboriginal Anthropology* (symposium papers). Australian Institute of Aboriginal Studies, Canberra, May 1968.

_____. "A Profile of Good and Bad in Australian Aboriginal Religion." In Robert B. Crotty ed., *The Charles Strong Lectures, 1972–1984.* Leiden: E. J. Brill, 1987.

_____. "Traditional Morality as Expressed through the Medium of an Australian Aboriginal Religion." *Australian Aboriginal Anthropology* 70: 216–247.

Bibby, Geoffrey. *Four Thousand Years Ago: A World Panorama of Life in the Second Millennium B. C.* New York: Knopf, 1961.

Biberi, Ion. "Man and the World of Values." *Ethnologica* ( Bucharest) 6, (1982): 102–113.

Bierhost, John. *The Sacred Path: Spells, Prayer and Power.* New York: William Morrow, 1983.

Binsbergen, Wim M .J. van. *Religious Change in Zambia: Exploratory Studies.* London-Boston: Kegan Paul International, 1981.

Birdwhistell, Ray L. "Background considerations to the Body as a Medium of 'Expression.'" In *The Body as a Medium of Expression.* London: A. Lane, 1975, 36–58.

Black Elk. *Black Elk Speaks.* Lincoln: University of Nebraska Press, 1961.

Bleek, D. F. "The Hadzapi of Watindega of Tanganyika Territory," *Africa* 4, no. 3 (July 1931): 273–286.

Bloch, Maurice, ed. *Political Language and Oratory in Traditional Society.* London- New York: Academic Press, 1975. Nebraska Press, 1989.

Blok, Anton. *The Mafia of a Sicilian Village, 1860–1960: A Study of Violent Peasant Entrepreneurs.* New York: Harper & Row, 1974.

Boaz, Franz. *Folk-Tales of Salishan and Sahaptin Tribes.* New York: Kraus Reprint, 1969.

Bob, Cecelia. Canim Lake Band, April and May 1991. Interview.

Bob, Norman. Canim Lake Band, April and May 1991. Interview.

Bognar, Carl J. "Self-Concept and Native Identity: Comparison of Four Communities in Labrador." *Journal of American Indian Education* 20, no. 2 (1981): 28–32.

Bohannan, Paul. "The Differing Realms of Law."In Paul Bohannan ed., *Law and Warfare; Studies in the Anthropology of Conflict.* Garden City, N.Y.: Natural History Press, 1967.

_____. *Justice and Judgment among the Tiv.* London-New York: Published for the International African Institute by Oxford University Press, 1957.

Boman, Thorleif. *Hebrew Thought Compared With Greek.* London: Student's Christian Union Press, 1960.

Bopp, Judie, et al. *The Sacred Tree.* Wilmot, Wisc.: Lotus Light, 1989.

Bouchard, Randy, and Dorothy Kennedy. *Shuswap Stories.* Vancouver: Commcept Publishing, 1979.

Bourdieu, Pierre. "The Sentiment of Honour in Kabyle Society." In Jean G. Peristiany, *Honour and Shame: The Values of Mediterranean Society.* Chicago: University of Chicago Press, 1966, 193–217.

Boyce, Mark (part-time resident at Canim Lake). Canim Lake Band, May and June 1991. Interview.

Brauer, Jerald C., ed. *The Lively Experiment Continued.* Macon, Ga: Mercer University Press, 1987.

Brenneis, Donald Lawrence, and Fred R. Myers. *Dangerous Words: Language and Politics in the Pacific.* New York: New York University Press, 1984.

Brislin, Richard W. "Cross-Cultural Research Methods." In Irwin Altman, Amos Rapoport, and Joachim F. Wohlwill, eds.. *Human Behavior and Environment,* Vol. 4. New York: Plenum Press, 47–81, 1980.

_____. *Cross-Cultural Encounters, Face-to-Face Interaction*. New York: Pergamon Press, 1981.

_____. *Cross-Cultural Research Methods*. New York: J. Wiley, 1973.

_____. *Intercultural Interactions: A Practical Guide*. Beverly Hills, Calif.: Sage Publications, 1986.

Brody, Hugh. *Maps and Dreams*. Vancouver: Douglas & McIntyre, 1981.

Brow, Catherine Judith. *"A Socio-Cultural History of the Alkali Lake Shuswap, 1882–1900."* University of Washington, Spokane, M. A. thesis, 1967.

Brown, Joseph Epes. *The Spiritual Legacy of the American Indian*. New York: Crossroad, 1982.

Brown, Thomas. *The Vision*. New York: Berkeley, 1988.

Buber, Martin. *Moses*. Oxford: East and West Library, 1946.

Bunker, S. "Dependency, Inequality and Development Policy: A Case from Bugisu, Uganda." *British Journal of Sociology* 34, no. 2 (1983): 182–207.

_____. "Center-Local Stuggles for Bureaucratic Controls in Bufisu, Uganda." *American Ethnologist* 10, no. 4 (1983): 749–69.

_____. "Ideologies of Intervention: The Ugandan State and Local Organisations in Bugisu." *Africa* 54, no. 3 (1984): 50–71.


Callicott, J. Baird. *In Defense of the Land Ethic: Essays in Environmental Philosophy*. Albany: State University of New York Press, 1989.

Campbell, Joseph. *Myths, Dreams and Religion*. New York: E. H. Dutton, 1970.

Canim Lake Gonzaga University Program. *Cultural Traditions of the Canim Lake Reserve* (bound pamphlet). Canim Lake, B.C.: Canim Lake Gonzaga University Program, 1991.

Carrington, John F. *Talking Drums of Africa*. London: Carcy Kingsgate Press, 1949.

Charlie, Rita. Canim Lake Band, April and May 1991. Interview.

Christopher, Charlotte. Canim Lake Band, May and June 1991. Interview.

Christopher, Fred. Canim Lake Band, May and June 1991. Interview.

Churchward, James. *The Lost Continent of Mu*. London: Neville Spearman, 1959.

Clark, Grahame. *World Prehistory and Natural Science*. Kobenhavn: Kommissionaer Munksgaard, 1980.

Clark, W. P. *The Indian Sign Language*. Lincoln: University of Nebraska Press, 1982.

Codrington, R. C. *The Melanesian Studies in Their Anthropology and Folklore*. Oxford: Clarendon Press, 1957.

Coffey, J., E. Goldstrom, G. Gottfriedson, R. Matthew, and P. Walton. *Shuswap History: The First 100 Years of Contact*. Kamloops: Secwepemc Cultural Education Society, 1990.

Collier, John. *Indians of the Americas: A Bibliography*. New York: W. W. Norton, 1947.

Cooper, B. "The Kindiga." *Tanganyika Notes and Records* 27 (June 1949): 8–15.

Cooper, Thomas W., Clifford G. Christians, Robert A. White, and Francis F. Plude. *Communication Ethics and Global Change.* White Plains, N.Y.: Longman, 1989.

Curtis, Natalie, ed. *The Indians' Book.* New York: Bonanza, 1987.

Danaher, Mary Alice (non-Native). Canim Lake Band, May and June 1991. Interview.

_____. *The Negotiation of Meaning in the Planning of a Degree Program in Indian Leadership.* Spokane: Gonzaga University, 1990.

Daniels, Ike. Canim Lake Band, April and May 1991. Interview.

Deloria, Vine, Jr., and Ralph Scissons, eds., "Theology, Law and American Indians." Paper presented at the Indian Law and Theology Symposium, Princeton Theology Seminar, December 14–16, 1983.

Demott, John. Memphis, Tennessee, February 1991. Interview.

Deng, Francis. *The Dinka People of the Sudan.* New York: Ablex, 1993.

Devine, George, ed. *A World More Human, a Church More Christian.* New York: Alba House, 1973.

Dick, Sheila. Canim Lake Band, May and June 1991. Interview.

Dike, Azuka A. *The Resilience of Igbo Culture: A Case Study of Awka Town.* Enugu, Nigeria: Fourth Dimension Publishers, 1985.

Dixon, Alana. Canim Lake Band, May and June 1991. Interview.

Dixon, Eddie. Canim Lake Band, April and May 1991. Interview.

Dixon, May. Canim Lake Band, April and May 1991. Interview.

Doblhofer, Ernst. *Voices in Stone: The Decipherment of Ancient Scripts and Writings.* Viking reprint editions. Clifton, N. J.: A. M. Kelley, 1973.

Douglas, M. "Techniques of Sorcery Control in Central Africa" In J. Middleton and E. H. Winter, eds., Witchcraft and Sorcery in East Africa. London: Routledge & Kegan Paul, 1963, 123–142.

Drucker, Philip. *Indians of the Northwest Coast.* Garden City, N.Y.: Natural History Press, 1955.

_____. *Culture of the North Pacific Coast.* San Francisco: Chandler, 1966.

Eastman, Carol M. "Establishing Social Identity Through Language Use." *Journal of Language and Social Psychology* 4, no. 2 (1985): 1–20.

Edel, May. *Anthropology and Ethics: The Quest for Moral Understanding.* Cleveland: Press of Case Western Reserve University, 1968.

Edmunds, Lowell. "Necessity, Chance and Freedom in the Early Atomists." *Phoenix* 26 (Winter 1972): 342–357.

Ekman, Paul. "Cross-Cultural Studies of Facial Expression." In *Darwin and Facial Expression: A Century of Research in Review.* New York: Academic Press, 1973, 44.

El-Hakim, Sherif. "The Structure and Dynamics of Consensus Decision-Making." In P. Loizos, ed., *Man: The Journal of the Royal Anthropological Institute* 13, no. 1. London: Royal Anthropologic Institute, March 1978.

Eliade, Mircea. *From Primitives to Zen: A Thematic Source Book of the History of Religions.* New York: Harper & Row, 1974.

_____. *Myths, Dreams, and Mysteries: The Encounter Between Contemporary Faith and Archaic Realities.* London: Harvill Press, 1960.

_____. *Man and the Sacred: A Thematic Source Book of the History of Religions.* New York: Harper & Row, 1974.

_____. *Patterns in Comparative Religion.* New York: Sheed & Ward, 1958.

_____. *Shamanism: Archaic Techniques of Ecstacy.* Princeton: Princeton University Press, 1974.

Emerson, Thomas I. "Communication and Freedom of Expression." *Scientific American* 227, no. 3 (1972): 163–172.

Emile, Gary. Canim Lake Band, May and June 1991. Interview.

Erasmus, Cynthia Chambers. "Ways with Stories: Listening to the Stories Aboriginal People Tell." *Language-Arts* 66, no. 3 (March 1989): 267–275.

Evans, Mary Augusta Tappage. *The Days of Augusta.* Seattle: Madrona Publishers, 1977.


Fagan, Brian M. *People of the Earth: An Introduction to World Prehistory.* New York: Harper Collins, 1992.

Falk-Moore, Sally. *Power and Property in Inca Peru.* New York: Columbia University Press, 1958.

_____. *Law as Process: An Anthropological Approach.* Boston: Routledge & Kegan Paul, 1984.

Farella, John R. *The Main Stalk: a Synthesis of Navajo Philosophy.* Tucson: University of Arizona Press, 1984.

Feleppa, Robert. *Convention, Translation, and Understanding: Philosophical Problems in the Comparative Study of Culture.* Albany: State University of New York Press, 1988.

Ferea, William. "On the Phenomena of Myths in Primal Religions: With Special Reference to Melanesia." Paper presented at the Workshop on Primal Spirituality, East-West Center, Honolulu, January 15, 1991.

Ferea, William. Honolulu, East–West Center January 1991. Interview.

Fiordo, Richard. "The Soft-Spoken Ways vs. The Outspoken Way: A Bicultural Approach to Teaching Speech Communication to Native People in Alberta." *Journal of American Indian Education* 24, no. 3 (July 1985): 5–48.

Fontmani, Louise. "Locality and Custom: Non-Aboriginal Claims to Customary Rights as a Form of Social Protest." *Journal of Rural Studies* 6, no. 2 (1990):195–208.

Ford, D. "The Anthropological Approach in Social Science." *The Advancement of Science* 4, no. 15 (September 1947): 213–224.

Ford, Weller, and Hector Muñoz. *Methodological Progress and Snags in Socialinguistic Field Research.* Mexico: Instituto of Superior Interpretes & Traductores, 1990.

Fortes, Meyer, ed. *African Political Systems.* London: Published for the International African Institute by Oxford University Press, 1950.

_____. *Kinship and the Social Order: The Legacy of Lewis Henry Morgan.* Chicago: Aldine, 1969.

Foucault, Michel. *Discipline and Punish: The Birth of the Prison.* New York: Vintage Books, 1979.

Fox, James J. ed. *The Flow of Life: Essays on Eastern Indonesia.* Cambridge: Harvard University Press, 1980.

_____. *To Speak in Pairs: Essays on the Ritual Languages of Eastern Indonesia.* Cambridge: Cambridge University Press, 1988.

Frank, Jim. Canim Lake Band, April and May 1991. Interview.

Frank, Mary Agnes. Canim Lake Band, April and May 1991. Interview.

Freud, Sigmund. *Basic Works.* Ed. William Strachery, Vol. 3. Franklin Center, Penn.: Franklin Library, 1978.

Friesen, Steven ed. *Local Knowledge, Ancient Wisdom: Challenges in Contemporary Spirituality.* Honolulu: Institute of Culture and Communication, East-West Center, 1991.

Fronval, George, and Daniel Dubois. *Indian Signals and Sign Languages.* New York: Bonanza, 1978.

Fry, Charles. "Natural Moral Law in the Blent of Cultural Relativism and Evolutionism." *Anthropological Quarterly* 34, no. 4 (1967): 177–191.

Fuller, E. G. *Salish and Kootenai Tribes: Anthropology and Tribal History.* New York: Clearwater Publishing, 1987.


Galanter, Mari. "Justice in Many Rooms: Courts, Private Ordering and Indigenous Law." *Journal of Legal Pluralism* 19 (1981): 1–47.

Gamble, Clive. *Information Exchange in the Paleolithic.* New York: Macmillan Journals, 1980.

Gardner, P.M. "Symmetric Respect and Memorate Knowledge: The Structure and Ecology of Individualistic Culture." *Southwestern Journal of Anthropology* 22, no. 4 (Winter 1966): 389–415.

Gardner, Robert. Harvard University, September 1990. Interview.

Geertz, Clifford "The Rotating Credit Association: A Middle-Rung in Development." *Economic Development and Cultural Change,*10: 241–263.

_____. *Local Knowledge: Further Essays in Interpretive Anthropology.* New York: Basic Books, 1983.

_____. *The Interpretation of Cultures: Selected Essays.* New York: Basic Books, 1973.

Gerbner, George, and Marsha Siefert, eds. *World Communications, A Handbook.* New York: Longman, 1984.

Girard, Rafael. *Esotericism of the Dopol Vuh.* London: Routledge and Kegan Paul, 1964.

Girienoz, Virgilio G., ed. *Indigenous Psychology.* Diliman, Philippines: New Horizons Press, 1990.

Glapp, John. *The Structure of a Native Moral Code.* Cambridge: Harvard University Press, 1957.

Gluckman, Max. *The Judicial Process among the Barotse of Northern Rhodesia.*

Manchester: Published for the Institute for Social Research, University of Zambia, by Manchester University Press, 1967.

_____. *The Ideas In Barotse Jurisprudence.* New Haven: Yale University Press, 1965, 242–272.

Goffman, Erving. *Forms of Talk.* Philadelphia: University of Pennsylvania Press, 1981.

_____. *Relations in Public: Microstudies of the Public Order.* New York: Basic Books, 1971.

Gordon, Cyrus Herzl. *Forgotten Scripts: How They Were Deciphered and Their Impact on Contemporary Culture.* New York: Basic Books, 1968.

Gordon, Robert J. *Law and Order in the New Guinea Highlands: Encounters with Enga.* Hanover, N.H.: Published for the University of Vermont by University Press of New England, 1985.

Griffin, Nicholas. "Aboriginal Rights: Gauthier's Arguments for Despoilation," *Dialogue* 20 (December 1981): 690–696.

Grim, John. Honolulu, East–West Center, January 1991. Interview.

Gumperz, John Joseph, and Dell H. Hymes. *Directions in Sociolinguistics: The Ethnography of Communication.* Oxford: Basil Blackwell, 1986.

Gumperz, John Joseph. *Discourse Strategies.* Cambridge: Cambridge University Press, 1982.

_____. *Language and Social Identity.* Cambridge: Cambridge University Press, 1982.

Gunther, Erna. Indian Life on the Northwest Coast of North America, as Seen by the Early Explorers and Fur Traders during the Last Decades of the Eighteenth Century. Chicago: University of Chicago Press, 1972.

Hailey, William Malcolm Hailey, Baron. *Native Administration in the British African Territories.* London: H.M. Stationery Office, 1950–1953.

Hall, Edward T., Jr. "Recent Clues to Athapascan Prehistory in the Southwest." *American Anthropologist* 46 (1944): 98–106.

Hall, Edward Twichell. *The Dance of Life: The Other Dimension of Time.* Garden City, N.Y.: Anchor Press/Doubleday, 1983.

Hanes, Johnny. "He was a Good Sport, a Good Loser." William Lake, *The Tribune,* June 5, 1980, 18.

Harris, Stephen. *Culture and Learning: Tradition and Education in North-East Arnhem Land.* Canberra: Australian Institute of Aboriginal Studies-Atlantic Highlands, N.J.: Humanities Press [distributor], 1984.

Harry, Laura. Alkali Lake, April and May 1991. Interview.

Hawthorn, Audrey. *People of the Potlatch.* Vancouver: Vancouver Art Gallery, 1957.

Headland, Thomas N., Kenneth L. Pike and Marvin Harris, eds. *Emics and Etics: The Insider/Outsider Debate.* Newbury Park, Calif.: Sage, 1990.

Heald, S. "Chiefs and Administrators in Bugisu." In A. F. Robertson, ed., *Uganda's First Republic: Chiefs, Administrators and Politicians, 1967–1971,* 76–98.

_____. "The Making of Men: The Relevance of Vernacular Psychology to the Interpretation of a Gisu Ritual," *Africa* 52, no.1 (1982): 15–36.

_____. "The Ritual Use of Violence: Circumcision among the Gisu of Uganda," in D. Riches, ed., *The Anthropology of Violence*. Oxford: Basil Blackwell, 70–85.

_____. "Witches and Thieves: Deviant Motivations in Gisu Society." *Man* 21, no. 1 (1986): 65–78.

Heider, Karl G. Grand Valley Dani, *Peaceful Warriors*. Fort Worth: Holt, Rinehart and Winston, 1991.

Heinberg, Richard. Corona, California, January 1991. Interview.

_____. Loveland, Colorado, August 1990. Interview.

_____. *Memories and Visions of Paradise: Exploring the Universal Myth of a Lost Golden Age*. Los Angeles: J. P. Tarcher, 1989.

Helm, June. *Indians of the Subartic: A Critical Bibliography*. Bloomington: Indiana University Press, 1976.

Helu, Futa. Honolulu, East–West Center, January 1991. Interview.

Hertzberg, Lars, and Juhani Pietarinen, eds. *Perspectives on Human Conduct*. Leiden New York: E. J. Brill, 1988.

Hiae, R. A., ed. "The Comparative Study of Non-Verbal Communication." In *The Body as a Medium of Expression: Essays Based on a Course of Lectures Given at the Institute of Contemporary Arts*, ed. Jonathan Benthall and Ted Polhemus.London: Allen Lane, 1975, 107–140.

Hiatt, Les. Harvard University, September 1990. Interview.

Hill-Tout, C. *British North America. Vol. 1., The Far West, the Home of the Salish and Dene*. London: Archibald Constable, 1907.

Hinde, R. A., ed. *Non-Verbal Communication*. Cambridge: University Press, 1972.

Hobsbawm, Eric J. *Primitive Rebels: Studies in Archaic Forms of Social Movement in the Nineteenth and Twentieth Centuries*. Manchester: Manchester University Press, 1959.

Hobson, Sarah. *Family Web: A Story of India*. Chicago: Academy Chicago, 1982.

Hoffman, Virginia. *Navajo Biographies*. Vol. 1. Rough Rock, Ariz.: Rough Rock Demonstration School, 1974.

*Holy Bible. King James text. Modern Phrased Version*. Oxford ed. New York: Oxford University Press, 1980.

Hopa, Ngapare. Honolulu, East–West Center, January 1991. Interview.

Humphreys, Sally. "Law as Discourse." *History and Anthropology* 1 (1985): 241–264.

Ii, John Papa. *Fragments of Hawaiian History*. Honolulu: Bishop Museum Press, 1983.

Innis, Harold, *The Bias of Communication*. Toronto: University of Toronto Press, 1951.

_____. *Empire and Communication,* Toronto: University of Toronto Press, 1952.
Irwin, James. *An Introduction to Maori Religion: Its Character before European Contact and Its Survival in C ontemporary Maori and New Zeal and Culture.* Bedford Park, S. Australia: Australian Association for the Study of Religions, 1984.

Jakubowicz, Andrew. "Indigenous Media in Australia: Aborigines and Torres Strait Islanders in the Australian Media." Paper presented at the IAMCR International Conference, Sao Paulo, 16– 23 August 1992.
James, A. Tett. "Sign Language of the Salishan Tribes of the Western Plateaus," In D. Jean Umriker-Sebeok and Thomas Sebeok, eds., Aboriginal Sign Languages of the Americas and Australia. New York: Plenum Press, 1978, vol. II, 77–90.
Jamin, Jean. *Les Lois du Silence: Essai Sur la Fonctin Sociale de Secret Dossiers Africains.* Paris: F. Maspero, 1977.
Jenness, Diamond. *The Indians of Canada.* Toronto: University of Toronto Press, in association with Ottawa, National Museum of Man, National Museum of Canada and Publishing Center, 1977.
Jennings, Jesse D., ed. *Ancient Native Americans.* San Francisco: W. H. Freeman, 1978.
Ji, John Papa. *Fragments of Hawaiian History.* Trans. M. K. Pukui. Honolulu: Bishop Museum Press, 1983.
Jimmy, Mandy (University of British Columbia). "Salishan Languages and Shuswap," Lecture at Gonzaga University, 1991. Program, Canim Lake Band, British Columbia, Canim Lake Shuswap Reserve, April 1991. Interview.
Jimmy, Mandy. Lecture, "The Salish Languages." Canim Lake Reserve, British Columbia, May 1991.
Johannesen, Richard L. *Ethics in Human Communication.* 2d ed. Prospect Heights, Ill.: Waveland Press, 1983.
Johnson, Amelia. Alkali Lake, April and May 1991. Interview.
Johnson, Becca, 100 Mile House, British Columbia, May 1991. Interview.
Johnson, Bruce, and Roberto Maestas. *Wasi'chu: The Continuing Indian Wars.* New York: Monthly Review Press, 1979.
Johnson, Fred. Alkali Lake, May and June 1991. Interview.
Johnson, Hazel. Alkali Lake Band, April and May 1991. Interview.
Johnson, Johnny. Alkali Lake Band, May and June 1991. Interview.
Johnson, Juliana. Alkali Lake Band, May and June 1991. Interview.
Johnson, Rubellite K. "The Hawaiian Kinolau: Manifestations of Deity in the Natural and Spiritual World." Paper presented at the Workshop on Primal Spirituality, East-West Center, Institute of Culture and Communication, University of Hawaii-Manoa, January 14, 1991.
_____. Honolulu, East–West Center, January 1991. Interview.
Jung, Carl. *The Archetypes of the Collective Subconscious.* Princeton, N.J.: Princeton University Press, 1934, 1969.

Kaeppler, Adrienne L. "Movement in the Performing Arts of the Pacific
    Islands: Dance." In Bob Fleshman, ed., *Theatrical Movement: A
    Bibliographical Anthology.* Metuchen, N.J.: Scarecrow Press, 1986.
Karp, Ivan. "Beer Drinking and Social Experience in an African Society: An
    Essay in Formal Sociology." In Ivan Karp and Charles S. Bird,eds.,
    *Explorations in African Systems of Thought.* Bloomington: Indiana
    University Press, 1980, 83–119.
Katz, Jane B. *We Rode the Wind.* Minneapolis: Leaner Publishing, 1975.
Keil, Carl Friedrich. *Biblical Commentary on the Old Testament.* Grand
    Rapids, Mich.: Eerdmans, 1949.
Kelsey, Jane. *A Question of Honor? Labour and the Treaty 1984–1989.* Boston:
    Allen & Unwin, 1990.
Kendon, Adam, ed. *Nonverbal Communication, Interaction and Gesture:
    Selections from Semiotica .* The Hague: Mouton Publishers, 1981.
Kerri, J. N. "Studying Voluntary Associations as Adaptive Mechanisms: A
    Review of Anthropological Perspectives." *Current Anthropology* 17, no. 1
    (1976): 25–47.
Kim, Young Yun. *Communication and Cross-Cultural Adaptation: An
    Integrative Theory.* Clevedon [England]-Philadelphia: Multilingual
    Matters, 1988.
Kluckhohn, Clyde. "Ethical Relativity: Sic Et Non," *Journal of Philosophy,* 53,
    (1955): 663–677.
_____. *The Navaho.* Cambridge: Harvard University Press-London, Oxford
    University Press, 1946.
_____. "Covert Culture and Administrative Problems." *American
    Anthropologist* 45 (1943): 213– 2 2 7.
_____. "A Navajo Personal Document." Southwestern Journal of Anthropology
    1 (1945): 260–283.
Kluckhohn, Clyde, and Dorothea Leighton. *The Navaho.* Cambridge: Harvard
    University Press, 1946, 1962.
Kohl-Larsen, L. *Wildbeuter in Ostafrika, die Tindiga, ein Jager und
    Sammlevolk.* Berlin: Dietrich Reimer, 1958.
Kramer, S. N. *Cradle of Civilization.* New York: Time, 1967.
Krober, A., and C. Kluckhohn. *Culture.* Cambridge: Papers of the Peabody
    Museum 37, no. 1 (1952).
Kroebal, A. L. "The Morals of Uncivilized People." *American Anthropology:*
    12, 437–447.
Kuipers, Bert H. *The Shuswap Language.* Paris: Mouton, 1974.
Kuoaloha, Elizabeth. Honolulu, University of Hawaii, February 1991. Interview.

La Fontaine, J. S. "The Gisu." In Audrey Isabel Richards, ed., *East African
    Chiefs; A Study of Political Development in Some Uganda and Tanganyika
    Tribes.* New York, Praeger, 1959, 260–277.
Ladd, John. *The Structure of a Moral Code: A Philosophical Analysis of Ethical*

*Discourse Applied to the Ethics of the Navajo Indians.* Cambridge: Harvard University Press, 1957.

Lamphere, Louise. "Symbolic Elements in Navajo Ritual." *Journal of Anthropology* 25 (1969): 279– 305.

Leach, Edmund Roland. Culture & Communication: *The Logic by which Symbols Are Connected: An Introduction to the Use of Structuralist Analysis in Social Anthropology.* Cambridge: Cambridge University Press, 1976.

Leighton, Alexander H., and Dorothea C. Leighton. "Elements of Psychotherapy in Navajo Religion." *Psychiatry,* 4 (1941): 515–524.

Leighton, Dorothea. *Children of the People.* Cambridge: Harvard University Press, 1947.

Leitch, Barbara. *Concise History of Indian Tribes.* Ottawa: Reference Publications, 1975.

León-Portilla, Miguel. *Aztec Thought and Culture: A Study of the Ancient Nahuatl Mind.* Norman: University of Oklahoma Press, 1963.

LePoer, Barbara A. *A Concise Dictionary of Indian Tribes of North America.* Algonac, Mich.: References Publications, 1979.

Lévi-Strauss, Claude. *The Savage Mind.* Chicago: University of Chicago Press, 1966.

_____. *The Way of Masks.* Seattle: University of Washington Press, 1982.

_____. *Tristes Tropiques.* New York: Atheneum, 1981.

Liberman, Kenneth. "Intercultural Communication in Central Australia." *Sociolinguistic Working Paper,* no. 104, Southwest Educational Development Lab, Austin, Texas, 1982.

Lippman, Walt. "Codes and Myths." in Jerome Davis, ed., *Readings in Sociology.* Boston: D. C. Heath, 1927.

Littleben, Thomas. Rockpoint Navajo Reserve, Rockpoint, Arizona, August 1990. Interview.

Long, Max Freedom. *Recovering the Ancient Magic.* Cape Girardeau, Mo.: Huna Press, 1978.

Lopez, Barry. "Renegotiating the Contracts: Mutual Obligation and Courtesies." *Parabola* 8, no. 2 (Spring 1983): 14–19.

Macaulay, Stewart. "Non-Contractual Relations in Business: A Preliminary Study." *American Sociological Review* 55 (February 1963): (offprint) 1–17.

MacBride, Sean. *Many Voices, One World: Communication and Society, Today and Tomorrow: The MacBride Report.* Paris: UNESCO, 1984.

Maestas, John, ed. *Contemporary Native American Address.* Salt Lake City: Brigham Young University Publishers, 1976.

Mahuta, R. T. *Commemorative Symposium on Race Relations in New Zealand: 150 Years after the Treaty of Waitangi.* Hamilton, New Zealand: Center for Maori Studies and Research, 1989.

Malafry, Hugh. Loveland Co., Colorado, August 1991. Interview.

Malcolm, Ian. "Speech Events of the Aboriginal Classroom," *International Journal of the Sociology of Language* 36 (1982):115–134.

Malinowski, Bronislaw. *Crime and Custom in Savage Society.* New York: Humanities Press, 1951.

\_\_\_\_. *The Foundations of Faith and Morals; An Anthropological Analysis of Primitive Beliefs and Conduct with Special Reference to the Fundamental Problems of Religion and Ethics.* London: Oxford University Press, H. Milford, 1936.

Malo, David. *Hawaiian Antiquities: Manuscript.* Bernice Pauahi Bishop Museum Library, Hawaiian Manuscript Collection, 1960.

Maori Economic Development Conference. *He Kawenata (Hui Taumata).* Department of Maori Affairs, Wellington, 1984.

Margold, Charles William. *Sex Freedom and Social Control.* Chicago: University of Chicago Press, 1926.

Mason, Michael C., and Georgina Fitzpatrick. *Religion in Australian Life: A Bibliography of Social Research.* Bedford Park, S. Australia: Australian Association for the Study of Religions, 1982.

Matt, Steve, Jr., Fund for Indian Education. *Salish and Kootenai Tribes Bibliography.* Dixon, Mont: Two Eagle River School, 1981.

McDonald, Henry. *The Normative Basis of Culture: A Philosophical Inquiry.* Baton Rouge: Louisiana State University Press, 1986.

McFeat, Tom. *Indians of the North Pacific Coast.* Seattle: University of Washington Press, 1967.

McLuhan, Marshall. *Understanding Media.* New York: McGraw-Hill, 1964.

Meeker, Lloyd. "Loveland Fireside Chats" (series of transcripts), 1944, N. P.

Meggitt, M. J. *Blood Is Their Argument: Warfare among the Mae Enga Tribesmen of the New Guinea Highlands.* Palo Alto, Calif.: Mayfield, 1977.

Mering, Otto von. *A Grammar of Human Values.* Pittsburgh: University of Pittsburgh Press, 1961.

Metge, J. A. *A New Maori Migration.* London: Athlone Press, 1964.

\_\_\_\_. *The Maori of New Zealand.* London: Routledge & Kegan Paul, 1967.

Metge, Joan. *Talking Past Each Other: Problems of Cross-Cultural Communication.* Wellington: Victoria University Press, 1978.

Michaels, Eric. "Constraints on Knowledge in an Economy of Oral Information." *Current Anthropology* 26, no. 4 (August-October 1985): 505–510.

\_\_\_\_. "The Right to Know and the Right to Show: Constraints on Knowledge in an Economy of Oral Information." Paper presented at the Annenberg Scholars Conference, February 1984.

Mills, George. *Navajo Art and Culture.* Colorado Springs: Taylor Museum of the Colorado Springs Fine Arts Center, 1959.

Mitchell, Charlie, and Benny Hale. *Alk'idaa' Adahoot'jjdii Beehaniihigii Baa Hane'.* (Memories of Old Stories.) Albuquerque : Navajo Reading Study , University of New Mexico, 1974.

Momaday, N. Scott. "A First American Views His Land." *National Geographic* (July 1976): 13–18, 294, 297.

\_\_\_\_. "Oral Tradition of the American Indian." In *Contemporary Native*

*American Address.* Ed. John Maestas. Salt Lake City: Brigham Young University, 1976.

Morgan, William. "The Organization of a Story and a Tale." *Journal of American Folk-Lore,* 58 (1945): 169–195.

Morice, Adrian Gabriel. *The History of the Northern Interior of British Columbia.* Smithers, B.C.: Interior Stationary, 1970.

Muller, Herbert Joseph. *Freedom in the Ancient World.* New York: Harper, 1961.

Munroe, Ruth H., Robert L. Munroe, and Beatrice B. Whiting. eds. *Handbook of Cross-Cultural Human Development.* New York: Garland STPM Press, 1981.

Murphy, Susan. "Communication in the Bush." *School Administrator* 41, no. 1 (29 January 1984): 11–12.

Nader, Laura. *Anthropology and the Law.* Mennshot, Wisc.: AAA, 1965.

Nance, John. Portland, Oregon, April 1989. Telephone interview.

_____. *The Gentle Tasaday: A Stone Age People in the Philippine Rain Forest.* New York: Harcourt Brace Jovanovich, 1975.

Naroll, Raoul. *A Handbook of Method in Cultural Anthropology.* [1st ed.]. Garden City, N.Y.: Published for the American Museum of Natural History by Natural History Press, 1970.

Naroll, Raoul. *The Moral Order: An Introduction to the Human Situation.* Beverly Hills: Sage Publications, 1983.

National Tribal Council. *The Shuswap: One People with One Mind, One Heart and One Spirit.* Kamloops: Shuswap National Tribal Council, 1989.

Neidjie, Bill, Stephen Davis, and Allan Fox. *Australia's Kakadu Man.* Darwin: Resource Managers, 1986.

Nichols, Claude Andrew. *Moral Education among the North American Indians.* New York: Bureau of Publishing, Columbia University, 1930.

Northrop, Filmer Stuart Cuckow, ed. *Cross-Cultural Understanding; Epistemology in Anthropology.* New York: Harper & Row, 1964.

Nottingham, Isla. "Land Economic Development and Cultural Survival: The New Zealand Maori." Paper read at the American Anthropology Association Meeting, Hamilton, New Zealand, Center for Maori Studies and Research, 1988.

O'Bryan, Aileen. *The Diné: Origin Myths of the Navajo Indians.* Smithsonian Institution, Bureau of American Ethnology. Washington, D.C.: Government Printing Office, 1956.

Obst, E. "Von Mkalama ins Land der Wakindiga." *Mitteilungen der Geogrphischen Gesellschaft in Hamburg* 26 (1912): 1–27.

Obuidho, Constance E. *Human Nonverbal Behavior: An Annotated Bibliography.* Westport, Conn.: Greenwood Press, 1979.

Okigbo, Charles. *World Communication Report.* Nairobi: African Council on Communication Education (for UNESCO), 1987.

____. "Modern Mass Communication Theories in the Context of African Communication." Paper presented at the Annual Conference of the International Communication Association, Honolulu, May, 1985.

Ontario Institute for Studies in Education. International Conference on Non-Verbal Behavior. New York: Alpalmic Press, 1979.

Orange, Claudia. *The Treaty of Waitangi*. Wellington, New Zealand: Allen & Unwin-Port Nicholson Press, 1987.

Palmer, Gary. "Persecution, Alliance, and Revenge in Shuswap Indian War Legends: A Formal Analysis." *Anthropological Papers*. Pocatello: Idaho Museum of Natural History, 1980.

Parkin, D. "Medicines and Men of Influence." *Man 3* (1968): 424–439.

Peek, Phillip. "The Power of Words in African Verbal Arts." *Journal of American Folklore* 94, no. 371 (1981): 19–41.

Pelto, Pertti J. *Anthropological Research: The Stucture of Inquiry*. New York: Harper & Row, 1970.

Pete, Elizabeth. Canim Lake Band, May and June 1991. Interview.

Pete, George. Canim Lake Band, May 1991. Interview.

Philips, Susan Urmston. *The Invisible Culture: Communication in Classroom and Community on the Warm Springs Indian Reservation*. New York: Longman, 1982.

Pike, Donald G. *Anasazi: Ancient People of the Rock*. Palo Alto, Calif.: American West, 1974.

Plato. *Phaedrus*. London: Whittaker; George Bell, 1868.

Polynesian Cultural Center, Exhibits of Authentic Polynesian Dance, tattoo, sculpture, crafts, (as documented by anthropologist Sergio Rapu), Oahu, 1991.

Porter, Frank W. *The Coast of Salish Peoples*. New York: Chelsea House, 1989.

Pospisil, Leopold J. *Anthropology of Law: A Comparative Theory*. New York: Harper & Row, 1971.

Preston, Scott. *Diné Bikeyah #18 — Alk'idaa' Oozei Asdiid Jini. (Navajo Land Series #18 — The Oraibi Massacre.)* Albuquerque: Navajo Reading Study, University of New Mexico, 1973.

Pritchard, James Bennett, ed. *The Ancient Near East: An Anthology of Texts and Pictures*. Princeton: Princeton University Press, 1958.

Rapu, Sergio. Polynesia Cultural Center, Oahu, Hawaii, January 11, 1991. Interview.

Reche, O. "Zur Ethnographie des Abflusslosen Gebietes Deutsch-Ostafrickas auf Grund der Sammlung der Ostafrika-expedition (Dr. E. Obst) der Feographischen Gesellschaft in Hamburg," *Abhanlungen des Hamburgischen Kolonialinstituts* 17 (1914): 5–23.

Reichard, Gladys A. *The Story of the Navajo Hail Chant*. New York: Published by the author, 1944.

_____. *Navajo Medicine Man.* New York: J. J. Augustin, 1939.

Richards, A. I. "A Modern Movement of Witch-Finders." *Africa* 8, no. 4 (1935): 448–461.

Riley, Carroll L., and Joni L. Manson. "Indian Spanish Communication Networks: Continuity in the Greater Southwest." Paper presented at the 81st Annual Meeting of the American Anthropological Association, Washington, D.C., 5 December 1982.

Ritchie, James E. *Working in the Maori World: Resource Papers.* Hamilton, New Zealand: Center for Maori Studies and Research, 1988.

_____. *Tribal Development in a Fourth World Context: The Maori Case.* Honolulu: East-West Center Association, 1990.

_____. Honolulu, East–West Center, January 1991. Interview.

Ritchie, James E., and Jane Ritchie. "Socialization." In Alan Howard and Robert Borofsky, *Developments in Polynesian Ethnology.* Honolulu: University of Hawaii Press, 1989.

Robbins, Ellen. Alkali Lake Band, April and May 1991. Interview.

Roberts, Helen H. *Musical Areas in Aboriginal North America.* Yale University Publications in Anthropology, no. 12 (New Haven: Yale University Press), 1936.

Rock Point Bilingual Education Project Title VII. *Diné Nooda'i Yil Anada'ahiijishchiigi. (War Between the Navajos and the Utes.)* Rock Point, Ariz., 1977.

Rock Point Community School. *Between Sacred Mountains: Stories and Lessons from the Land.* Chinle, Ariz.: Rock Point Community School, 1982.

Rogers, E.S. "The Shuswap." The Beaver, 300 (Spring 1970): 56-59.

Rose, Deborah Bird. "Aboriginal Australia." In North Ryde, ed., *The Australian People.* N.S.W.: Angus & Robertson, 1988.

_____. "Ethnobotany." *Aboriginal Health Worker* 12, no. 3 (1988): 21–25.

_____. "Ned Lives!" *Australian Aboriginal Study,* no. 2 (1989): 51–59.

_____. "Review of 'End of An Era: Aboriginal Labour in the Northern Territory.'" *Australian Aboriginal Study,* no. 1 (1988): 93–99.

Ruby, Robert H. *Indians of the Pacific Northwest: A History.* Norman: University of Oklahoma Press, 1981.

Ruffini, Julio L. "Disputing over Livestock in Sardinia." In Laura Nader and Harry F. Todd, Jr., eds., *The Disputing Process: Law in Ten Societies.* New York: Columbia University Press, 1978, chapter 7.

Rutter, Michael, and Nicola Madge. *Cycles of Disadvantage: A Review of Research.* London: Heinemann, 1976.

Rynkiewich, Michael A. and James P. Spradley, eds. *Ethics and Anthropology: Dilemmas in Fieldwork.* Malabar, Fla.: R. E. Krieger, 1976.

Sapir, Edward. *Navajo Texts.* Iowa City: Linguistic Society of America, 1942.

Savishinsky, Joel S. "Vicarious Emotions and Cultural Restraint." *Journal of Psychoanalytic Anthropology* 5, no. 2 (Spring 1982):115–135.

Schapera, Isaac. *Government and Politics in Tribal Societies.* London: Watts, 1956.

Schwartz, O Douglas. "Indian Rights and Environmental Ethics," *Environ Ethics* 9 (Winter 1987): 291–302.

Schwimmer, Eric. *The Maori People in the Nineteen Sixties.* Auckland: Blackwood and Janet Paul, 1968.

Scollon, Ron, and Suzanne Scollon. "Language Dilemmas in Alaska." *Society* 2, no. 4 (May-June 1983): 77–81.

Service, Elman Rogers. *Primitive Social Organization: An Evolutionary Perspective.* New York: Random House, 1962.

Shimanoff, Susan B. *Communication Rules: Theory and Research.* Beverly Hills, Calif.: Sage Publications, 1980.

Shopen, Timothy. *Languages and Their Speakers.* Cambridge, Mass.: Winthrop Publishers, 1979.

Shuswap National Tribal Council. *The Shuswap: One People with One Mind, One Heart, and One Spirit.* Kamloops: Shuswap National Tribal Council, 1989.

Siegel, Bernard J., Alan R. Beals and Stephen A. Tyler, eds., *Annual Review of Anthropology* 10. Palo Alto, Calif.: Annual Reviews, 1990.

Simmons, D. R. *The Great New Zealand Myth: A Study of the Discovery and Origin Traditions of the Maori.* Wellington: A. H. & A. W. Reed, 1976.

Smith, Alfred Goud, ed. *Communication and Culture: Readings in the Codes of Human Interaction.* New York: Holt, Rinehart and Winston, 1966.

Smith, Marian Wesley. *Indians of the Urban Northwest.* New York: Columbia University Press, 1949.

Smith, W. John. "Ritual and the Ethology of Communicating." In *The Spectrum of Ritual: A Biogenetic Stuctural Analysis,* by Eugene G. D'Aquili, Charles D. Laughlin, Jr., and John McManus. New York: Columbia University Press, 1979, 51–77.

Smith, Watson. *Zuni Law: A Field of Values.* Papers of the Peabody Museum of American Archaeology and Ethnology, Harvard University, vol. 43, no. 1. Reports of the Rimrock Project; Millwood, N.Y.: Kraus Reprint Co., 1973.

Smyly, John, and Carolyn Smyly. *Those Born at Koona.* Vancouver: Hancock, 1973.

Sondhi, Krishan. *Communication and Values.* Bombay: Somalya, 1985.

Sorokin, Pitrim Aleksandrovich. *Social and Cultural Dynamics: A Study of Change in Major Systems of Art, Truth, Ethics, Law and Social Relationships.* Boston: Porter Sergent, 1970.

Spahan, Mahdi (via Ellen Robbins). Alkali Lake Band, April and May 1991. Interview.

Speare, Jean, ed. *The Days of Augusta.* Seattle: Madrona Publishers, 1977.

Spencer, Herbert. *The Data of Ethics.* New York: D. Appleton, 1883.

Spencer, Katharine. *An Analysis of Navaho Chantway Myths.* Philadelphia: American Folklore Society, 1951.

Spicer, Edward H. *Cycles of Conquest.* Tucson: University of Arizona Press, 1962.

Sproul, Barbara C. *Primal Myths: Creating the World.* San Francisco: Harper & Row, 1979.

Squinahan, Lily. Alkali Lake Band, April and May 1991. Interview.

St. Cur, Princess Red Wing. "Indian Communications," *College Composition and Communication* 23, no. 5 (1976): 350–356.

Standing Bear, Luther. *Stories of the Sioux.* Lincoln: University of Nebraska Press, 1981.

Steinbauer, Friedrich. *Melanesian Cargo Cults: New Salvation Movements in the South Pacific.* St. Lucia: University of Queensland Press, 1979.

Steward, Julian Haynes. *Theory of Culture Change: The Methodology of Multilinear Evolution.* Urbana, University of Illinois Press, 1955.

Stokes, John. "Native and Aboriginal Men's Lore," Lectures at Minnesota Men's Gathering, Sturgeon Lake, Minnesota, September 6–9, 1991. Interview.

Stratbern, Andrew. "When Dispute Procedures Fail." In A. L. Epstein, ed., *Contention and Dispute: Aspects of Law and Social Control in Melanesia.* Canberra: Australian National University Press- Portland, Ore.: International Scholarly Book Services, 1974, chapter 7.

Sullivan, Lawrence E. "Above, Below or Far Away: Ancient Cosmogony and Ethical Order." In *Cosmogony and Ethical Order: New Studies in Comparative Ethics,* eds. Robin W. Lovin and Frank E. Reynolds. Chicago: University of Chicago Press, 1985, 98–129.

_____. *Healing and Restoring: Health and Medicine in the World's Religious Traditions.* New York: Macmillan-London: Collier Macmillan, 1989.

_____. "Sound and Senses: Toward a Hermaneutics of Performance." *History of Religions* 26, no. 1 (1986): 1–33.

_____. East–West Center, January 1991. Interview.

Sun Bear. New York, February 18, 1988. Interview.

Surtees, Robert J. *Canadian Indian Policy: A Critical Bibliography.* Bloomington: Indiana University Press, 1982.

Tatar, Elizabeth. *"Nineteenth-Century Hawaiian Chant."* Ph.D. dissertation, Department of Anthropology, Bernice P. Bishop Museum, 1982.

Teit, James A. *The Shuswap, Vol. 2, pt. 7, The Jesup North Pacific Expedition,* ed.Franz Boaz. New York: G. E. Thehert, 1909, 447–789.

_____. "Sign Languages of the Salishan Tribes of the Western Plateaus." *Aboriginal Sign Languages.* New York: Plenum Press, 1904, 2: 77–90.

Tempels, Placied. *Bantu Philosophy.* Paris: Presence Africaine, 1969.

Thayer, Lee. "Communication Systems." In *The Relevance of General Systems Theory: Papers Presented to Ludwig von Bertalanffy on His Seventieth Birthday,* ed. Ervin Laszlo. New York: G. Braziller, 1972.

Theodore, Elsie. Canim Lake Band, May and June 1991. Interview.

Thomas, Hilah Frances, and Rosemary Skinner Keller, eds. *Women in New Worlds: Historical Perspectives on the Wesleyan Tradition.* Nashville: Abingdon, 1981.

Tompkins, Peter. *Secrets of the Great Pyramid.* New York: Harper, 1971.

Toynbee, Arnold. *A Study of History.* New York: Oxford University Press, 1962.

Traber, Michael, ed. *The Myth of the Information Revolution: Social and Ethical Implications of Communication Technology.* Beverly Hills, Calif.: Sage Publications, 1986.

Triandis, Harry Charalambos. *Handbook of Cross-Cultural Psychology.* Boston: Allyn and Bacon, 1980.

Trigger, Bruce Graham. "Inequality and Communication in Early Civilizations." *Anthropologica* (Ottawa)18, no. 1 (1976): 27–52.

Trivers, Robert. *Social Evolution.* Menlo Park, Calif.: Benjamin/Cummings, 1985.

Turnbull, Colin M. *Wayward Servants: The Two Worlds of the African Pygmies.* Garden City, N.Y.: Published for the American Museum of Natural History by Natural History Press, 1965.

Tuza, E. "A Melanesian Cosmological Process." In H. Olela, ed., *Total Cosmic Vision of Life: An Introduction to Melanesian Philosophy.* Boroko, Papua New Guinea: Institute of Papua New Guinea Studies, 1981.

Ullman, Berthold Louis. *Ancient Writing and Its Influence: Our Debt to Greece and Rome.* New York: Cooper Square Publishers, 1963.

Umiker-Sebeok, D. Jean, and Thomas Sebeok, eds. *Aboriginal Sign Languages of the Americas and Australia.* New York: Plenum Press, 1978.

Underhill, Ruth Murray. Indians of the Pacific Northwest. Washington, D. C.: Department of the Interior, 1960.

_____. *The Navajos.* The Civilization of the American Indian Series, no. 43. Norman: University of Oklahoma Press, 1956.

Valkenburgh, Richard R. *Dine Vikeyah. (The Navajo Country).* Window Rock, Ariz.: U. S. Department of Interior, Office of Indian Affairs, 1941.

Van Duzen, Grace. Loveland, Colorado, August 1990. Interview.

Velikovsky, Immanuel. *Ages in Chaos.* Garden City: Doubleday, 1952.

_____. *Mankind in Amnesia.* London: Sidgwick & Jackson, 1982.

_____. *Worlds in Collision.* Garden City, N.Y.: Doubleday, 1950.

Vogy, Euonz. "Navajo." *In Perspectives in American Indian Culture Change.* Chicago: University of Chicago Press, 1961.

von Raffler-Engel, Walburga, ed. *Aspects of Nonverbal Communication.* Lisse: Swets and Zeitlinger, 1980.

_____. "The Protestant Ethic and the Spirit of Capitalism." In H. H. Gerth and C. W. Mills, eds., From Max Weber: *Essays in Sociology.* London: Routledge, 1991.

von Sturmer, J. "Talking with Aborigines." *Australian Institute of Aboriginal Studies Newsletter* 15 (1981).

Waters, Frank. *Book of the Hopi.* New York: Viking Press, 1963.

Watson-Gegeo, Karen Ann, and Geoffrey Miles White, eds. *Disentangling:*

*Conflict Discourse in Pacific Societies.* Stanford: Stanford University Press, 1990.

Weitz, Shirley. *Nonverbal Communication: Readings with Commentary.* New York, Oxford University Press, 1974.

Wescott, Roger. Massachusetts, New Jersey; September 1991. Telephone interview.

Westermarck, Edward. *The Origin and Development of the Moral Ideas.* London-New York: Macmillan, 1906–1908.

White, John Peter, Margrit Koettig, and James F. O'Connell. *A Prehistory of Australia, New Guinea, and Sahul.* Sydney-New York: Academic Press, 1982.

Whitten, Phillip, and David E. Hunter. *Anthropology, Contemporary Perspectives.* Glenview, Ill.: Scott, Foresman, 1990.

Williams, Nancy M. *The Yolngu and Their Land: A System of Land Tenure and the Fight for Its Recognition.* Stanford: Stanford University Press, 1986.

Willis, R. G. "Kamcape: An Anti-Sorcery Movement in Southwest Tanzania," *Africa* 38, no. 1 (1968):1–15.

_____. "Instant Millennium: The Sociology of African Witch-Cleansing Cults." In M. Douglas ed., *Witchcraft Confessions and Accusations.* London: Tavistock, 1970, 129–140.

Wilson Schaef, Anne. Kauai, Hawaii, February 1991. Interview.

Witherspoon, Gary. *Language and Art in the Navajo Universe.* Ann Arbor: University of Michigan Press, 1977.

_____. "A New Look at Navajo Social Organization." *American Anthropologist* 73 (1970): 55–65.

_____. "The Central Concepts of Navajo World View (1)." *Linguistics* 119 (January 1974): 41–59.

Wolf, Carolyn, and Karen Folk. *Indians of North and South America: A Bibliography.* New York: Scarecrow Press, 1977.

Woodburn, Jack. "Minimal Politics: The Political Organization of the Hadza of North Tanzania." In William A. Shack and Percy S. Cohen, eds., *Politics in Leadership: A Comparative Perspective.* Oxford: Clarendon Press-New York: Oxford University Press, 1979.

_____. "Social Change and Sedentarization among Hunters-Gatherers: Ecological and Political Factors." Paper read at the Social Science Research Council Symposium on "The Future of Traditional 'Primitive' Societies," Cambridge, England, December 1974.

_____. "An Introduction to Hadza Ecology." In R. B. Lee and I. DeVore, eds., *Man the Hunter.* Chicago: Aldine, 1968, 49–55.

_____. "Ecology, Nomadic Movement and the Composition of the Local Group Among Hunters and Gatherers: An East African Example and its Implications." in P. J. Ucko, R. Tringham, and G. W. Dimbleby, eds., *Man, Settlement and Urbanism.* London: Gerald Duckworth, 1972, 192–206.

_____. "Stability and Flexibility in Hadza Residential Groupings." In R. B. Lee and I. DeVore, eds., *Man the Hunter.* Chicago: Aldine, 1968, 103–110.

_____. *"The Social Organization of the Hadza of North Tanganyika."* Ph.D. dissertation, Cambridge University, 1964.

_____. *Hunters and Gatherers: The Material Culture of the Nomadic Hadza.* London: British Museum, 1970.

Woodburn, Jack, and J. Hudson, *The Hadza: The Food Quest of an East African Hunting and Gathering Tribe* (16 mm. Ethnographic Film), 1966.

Woodbury, Anthony C. "The Functions of Rhetorical Structure: A Study of Central Alaskan Yupik Eskimo Discourse." *Language in Society* 14, no. 2 (June 1985): 153–190.

Woodcock, George. *Peoples of the Coast: The Indians of the Pacific Northwest.* Bloomington: Indiana University Press, 1977.

Worsley, Peter. *The Trumpet Shall Sound: A Study of "Cargo" Cults in Melanesia.* New York: Schocken Books, 1968.

Worth, Sol, and John Adair. *Through Navaho Eyes.* Bloomington: Indiana University Press, 1972.

Wyman, Leland Clifton. *Blessingway.* Tucson: University of Arizona Press, 1970.

Young, Robert W., and William Morgan. *The Navajo Language.* Phoenix: Educational Division, Bureau of Indian Affairs, 1943.

Young, Thomas J., Charles LaPlante, and Webster Robbins. "Indians before the Law: An Assessment of Contravening Cultural/Legal Ideologies." *Quarterly Journal of Ideology* 11, no. 4 (1987): 59–70.

Zolbrod, Paul G. *Diné Bahane: The Navajo Creation Story.* Albuquerque: University of New Mexico Press, 1984.

## FILMS, VIDEOTAPES, AND TELEVISION PROGRAMS

"Buried Mirror: Conflict of the Gods" (videotape). 1991; PBS; 60 min.; VHS. Writer Carlos Fuentes traces the Aztec Indian world through ancient ruins and sculpture, and discusses the nature and consequences of the first encounter between the Spanish and the Indigenous people of America. V995.

*Dances with Wolves* (feature film). USA: 1990; 181 min.; VHS. Kevin Costner as a Civil War hero who learns the culture of the Sioux Indians. V1016.

"From the Heart of the World: The Elder Brother's Warning" (videotape). 1991; BBC-TV; 90 min.; VHS. Documentary on the Kogi people of Columbia. Calling themselves the elder brothers of the human race, they use this film as an opportunity to issue a warning to modern man about the balance of life on earth. V948.

"Interview with Tom Cooper," *Frontiers.* Boston: The Monitor Channel, The Christian Science Publishing Society, 1991. First aired Nov. 30, 1991.

*Little Big Man* (feature film). USA: 1970; 150 min.; VHS. A revisionist
  Western, based on the novel by Thomas Berger. Dustin Hoffman plays
  121-year-old Jack Crabb, whose past includes lives as a gunslinger, Indian,
  and survivor of Little Big Horn. V102.
"Live and Remember" (videotape). 1987; 29 min.; VHS. Documentary on the
  Lakota Sioux nation's oral tradition, song and dance, medicine, and
  spirituality. Opens with a look inside the seldom-recorded Lakota Sweat
  Lodge Ceremony. V979.
*Millennium: Tribal Wisdom and the Modern World* (videotape series). 1992;
  PBS; VHS. Ten tapes. Viewer's guide and other materials available.
____. "A Poor Man Shames Us All" (videotape). 1992; 60 min.; PBS; VHS.
  Looks at the views of wealth and economy exhibited in the lives of tribal
  cultures, including the Weyewa of Indonesia and the Gabra of Kenya. Also
  considers the impact of advertising on Western culture. V990G.
____. "An Ecology of the Mind" (videotape). 1992; 60 min.; PBS; VHS. Looks
  at the ways tribal cultures interact with nature; visits the Gabra of northern Kenya, the Makuma of Columbia, and a Canadian gardener. V990D.
____. "At the Threshold" (videotape). 1992; 60 min.; PBS; VHS. Examines the
  conflict between Western ideals of individual freedom and self-interest
  and tribal values of belonging and the primacy of the group. Focuses on
  the Xavante tribe of Brazil and the Navajo of the American Southwest.
  V990J.
____. "Inventing Reality" (videotape). 1992; 60 min.; PBS; VHS. Contrasts
  Western concepts of objective reality with tribal concepts of magic. Visits
  a Huichol Indian village battling an epidemic with traditional Western
  treatment, a Canadian cancer treatment center, and an Aboriginal elder.
  V990H.
____. "Mistaken Identity" (videotape). 1992; 60 min.; PBS; VHS. Explores
  issues of individual identity. Looks at the lives of a Canadian abortion
  counselor, a Xavante Indian boy, and an Indonesian tribesman. V990C.
____. "Strange Relations" (videotape). 1992; 60 min.; PBS; VHS. Looks at
  how tribal societies in Nepal and Niger deal with the conflict between
  romantic love and society's need for stable marriages. V990B.
____. "The Art of Living" (videotape). 1992; 60 min.; PBS; VHS. Explores the
  nature of art in the Wodaabe tribe of Niger, the Dogon of Mali, and in the
  ideas of a Western artist. V990E.
____. "The Shock of the Other" (videotape). 1992; 60 min.; PBS; VHS. Host
  David Maybury-Lewis visits his Xavante "brother," and journeys with the
  *Millennium* series crew into the Peruvian jungle to locate a tribe that
  remains hidden from the outside world. V990A.
____. "The Tightrope of Power" (videotape). 1992; 60 min.; PBS; VHS.
  Contrasts the Western forms of state with tribal practices of government.
  Focuses on the struggles of the Ojibwa-Cree and Mohawk tribes against
  the Canadian government. V990I.

_____. "Touching the Timeless" (videotape). 1992; 60 min.; PBS; VHS. Explores concepts of the sacred by following the Huichol tribe of Mexico on their annual pilgrimage to collect peyote, and visiting the home of a Navajo medicine man. V990F.

"More Than Bows and Arrows" (videotape). N. Scott Momaday; 1992; PBS; 60 min.; VHS. Writer Momaday hosts this documentary about the contributions of American Indians to the contemporary American culture. V992.

"My Hands are the Tools of My Soul" (film). Barron, Arthur; Voynow, Zina, directors/writers; 54 min.; 16mm. Illustrates the cultural landscape of Native Americans, using their pottery, music and dance, and everyday activity to reveal their sense of harmony between man and nature. F158.

*Mystery of the Red Paint People* (video). Public Broadcasting Series (PBS), n.p., c. 1989.

# Index